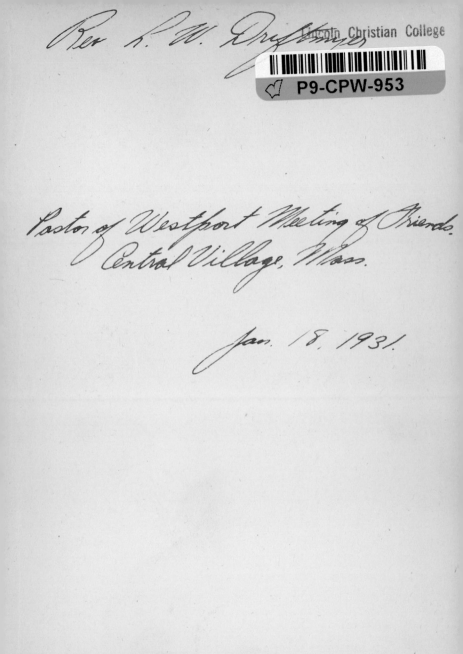

Rev. L. W. Dexsanger

Pastor of Westport Meeting of Friends.
Central Village, Mass.

Jan. 18, 1931.

CREATIVE LIVES

Edited by

HAROLD E. B. SPEIGHT, M.A., D.D.

~~~~~~~

GEORGE FOX

Seeker and Friend

✠

THE LELY PORTRAIT OF GEORGE FOX

Creative Lives

GEORGE FOX
SEEKER AND FRIEND

By

Rufus M. Jones, LL.D.

PROFESSOR OF PHILOSOPHY
IN HAVERFORD COLLEGE

1930
HARPER & BROTHERS PUBLISHERS
New York and London

92
F79j

N.Y.

CONTENTS

~~~~~~

~~~~~~

31087

Preface

George Fox was beyond question a vital personality and it is fitting that the story of his life should be included in the list of those who have been valiant for the truth and who have made an important contribution to the spiritual progress of the race. This Life of Fox has been written, not primarily for those who are his followers and disciples in name and faith, but rather for that wider group of persons who are only remotely acquainted with him as a seventeenth-century figure in leather breeches, the founder of the Quakers and an apostle of the divine in man. His best ideals have now become a part of the common air we breathe, but the bold champion of them in a time when they were novel and dangerous and costly deserves to be better known and to have his story brought up to date for general readers. There is a good short biography entitled George Fox by Dr. Thomas Hodgkin. There is an excellent little book by A. Neave Brayshaw, The

Personality of George Fox, *and there is a luminous treatment of him in William Charles Braithwaite's Beginnings of Quakerism. But there is still a place left open with the general modern reader for a new Life of the man who was in a very real sense the forerunner and champion of much that is vital in the religious thought of today. I want to express my appreciation for the help and suggestions I have received from that noted expert in all matters that connect with the life of Fox, Dr. Norman Penney of the Friends' Library in London.*

RUFUS M. JONES

Haverford,
Pennsylvania

George Fox, Seeker and Friend

CHAPTER I

The Occasion and the Man

THOMAS CARLYLE, in *Sartor Resartus*, declared in his rapturous manner, that George Fox was "one of those persons to whom, under ruder or purer form, the Divine Idea of the Universe is pleased to manifest itself." He is, Carlyle concludes, "the greatest of the moderns."

During the hundred years since Carlyle wrote his famous chapter on "An Incident in Modern History," which vividly described the young prophet cutting out his suit of leather, George Fox has been steadily growing in importance and significance in the minds of historians of religious movements and of students of spiritual biography. William James was hardly less enthusiastic than Carlyle in his appreciation of George Fox. "The Quaker religion," he says, "which he (Fox) founded is something which it is impossible to over-praise. In a day of shams,

[1]

it was a religion of veracity rooted in spiritual inwardness, and a return to something more like the gospel truth than men had ever known in England. . . . Every one who confronted him personally, from Oliver Cromwell down to county magistrates and jailers, seems to have acknowledged his superior power." [1]

Fox has emerged from his earlier position as the founder of a small sect and is now considered rather as the exponent of a fresh and significant type of mystical religion and practical-spiritual Christianity which widens out beyond the range and scope of any one sect or denomination. James says, probably with some exaggeration: "So far as our Christian sects today are evolving into liberality, they are simply reverting in essence to the position which Fox . . . so long ago assumed." [2]

It is interesting to discover in this connection that Fox never thought of himself as the founder of a sect. The breadth and universality of the religious principle which Fox discovered, or rather rediscovered, are everywhere in evidence in his messages and in his writings. He lived and laboured in the hope and

[1] *Varieties of Religious Experience*, p. 7.
[2] *Ibid.*, p. 7.

[2]

belief that he was to be an instrument in the hands of God for the restoration of apostolic Christianity to its primitive freshness, vitality, and power. It was not a new sect, or a new Protestant denomination, which he believed he was sent to found, but he conceived rather that he and his band of followers were the "seed" of the new and universal Church of Christ, brought back at last from its wanderings in the wilderness and revivified by the real presence of its divine Head. Thomas Hancock, in his scholarly monograph, *The Peculium* (London, 1859; Philadelphia, 1860), has produced an impressive array of evidence to the effect that the original Quaker idea was the inauguration of a spiritual movement that was no less ambitious in its scope than the recovery and recreation of the universal Church of Christ.

George Fox was weak in historical perspective, as most would-be restorers of primitive perfections have been both before and since his day. He over-estimated, too, the originality and the creative organizing power of his discovery and his principle, but when all discounts have been made he stands forth after three hundred years as a sterling, sincere, honest man, as a true prophet of spiritual religion and as a rugged, fascinating personality, to whom the world will almost certainly again and again return in coming years for light and leading.

It is a well-recognised fact that the English Reformation was carried through in the reigns of Henry VIII, Edward VI, and Elizabeth without the guiding power of any outstanding spiritual hero. There were noble martyrs and there were men of large capacity in statesmanship. But there was no major prophet who by inspiration, conviction, and illuminated vision could lift his nation to a new table-land of truth and experience. The increase of religious depth and fervour came to the English people only slowly and gradually, long after Luther and Calvin had wrought their powerful work of faith and insight in the hearts of their fervent followers. No one can read the story of the religious confusions which prevailed in England for the hundred years which followed the Act that made Henry VIII the Head of the Church without wondering why no spiritual genius appeared in those years of crisis to alter the line of march for the English race and to do for religion what Shakespeare did for literature. As a result of this failure, the spiritual reformation had to come piecemeal and in stages rather than in one glorious burst of transformation. George Fox came on the scene after the Puritan movement had slowly ripened conviction and had produced a notable increase of spiritual depth in men's souls. He came, too, after the idea of democracy and self-government in the affairs of religion had been widely promulgated by Anabaptists and Independents. And he thus came to his task at a moment when the occasion was ripe for a fresh forward movement. The field was prepared and was waiting for the seed. Fox's prophetic genius is revealed in the way in which he had the intuition and insight to see what the times demanded and to cast into the prepared ground the seed that was peculiarly suited for that occasion and for that soil. He takes his place in history among the religious reformers, and the principle of life which he promulgated must be judged, as Luther's announcement of *faith* must be, by the way in which it ministered to a new and higher stage in the history of man's spiritual progress.

CHAPTER II

Childhood, Youth, and Mystical Experience

FENNY DRAYTON, the birthplace of George Fox, is in the heart of the Midlands, from which have come many of the great personalities of English history. It is a small hamlet in Leicestershire, about four miles from Nuneaton, the birthplace and early home of George Eliot. The region is low and flat, with gently rising ground toward the east and with the hills of Atherstone in view toward the west. Fox calls his hamlet "Drayton-in-the-Clay," and it was literally clay or fen country in the seventeenth century, but good drainage has now brought it under excellent cultivation and given it a genuine charm and simple beauty. While the general region has changed for the better, the hamlet itself has moved in the opposite direction and has lost the attractiveness of its earlier Jacobean homes.

Here, in July, 1624, Fox was born of humble

but "honest and sufficient," parents. The second part of this quoted phrase, which is taken from William Penn, signifies that the family was well removed from poverty and was in comfortable standing. Fox himself leaves no doubt in his *Journal* about the genuine quality of his father and mother. The former, he says, was a weaver, an honest man, whom the neighbours called "Righteous Christer" (Christopher) and the son adds proudly, "there was a seed of God in him." [1]

"My mother," the simple, straightforward account says, "was an upright woman; her maiden name was Mary Lago, of the family of the Lagos, and of the stock of the martyrs." The martyred ancestor was probably a member of the Glover family of Mancetter, which is a few miles north of Drayton, on the old Watling Street of Roman times. It is interesting to note how differently Bunyan refers to his family, always with marked depreciation. "My descent was of a low and inconsiderable generation," he writes in *Grace Abounding*, "my father's house being of that rank that is meanest and most despised of all families of the land."

[1] George Fox's *Journal* (bi-centenary edition, London, 1901), p. 1.

[7]

There is no record in the Drayton parish register either of the birth or of the baptism of the child, and the actual day of his birth in July remains uncertain. Many pages of the register at just this critical period about which we want facts are missing, though the baptism of George's sister, Dorothy, is duly recorded under date of April 9, 1626. It is an interesting fact that he was born the same year that Jacob Boehme, one of his most direct spiritual ancestors, died in Silesia. Boehme kindled his torch from the flame of the spiritual reformers of the sixteenth century, and he in turn, dying in 1624, helped to light the new flame that was to kindle many more torches through the years. John Everard, who was the foremost English transmitter of the message of the spiritual reformers on the Continent, was forty-nine years old when Fox was born, and was faithfully preparing the soil for the seed which this new-born child from Drayton was in maturer years to scatter broadcast. King James I had one more year to live, and Prince Charles was about to enter into marriage with Henrietta Maria, the daughter of the great Henry of Navarre. The forces were slowly shaping to produce the conditions of the Commonwealth period, out of which Fox's movement would emerge.

There can be no question that the influences of the humble Drayton home were the essential environment for the formation of the inner life of Fox. William Penn says that his mother was "accomplished above most of her degree in the place where she lived," and all of Fox's references to his mother are tender and affectionate. The home, like that of Martin Luther, was penetrated with an atmosphere of pure and undefiled religion. Sobriety and simplicity, honesty and honour, sincerity and truth, reverence and respect, were incarnated in the lives of these two persons who brought forth and nurtured this child that was destined to be a religious prophet and reformer. "In my very young years," he says, "I had gravity and stayedness of mind and spirit not usual in children." "When I came to eleven years of age I knew pureness and righteousness; for while a child I was taught how to walk to be kept pure." [1]

That is a beautiful testimony to the creative spiritual nurture of a home. When he says that he was "taught how to walk to be kept

[1] *Journal*, p. 2.

pure," he is quite probably referring to an inward and divine teaching, but even if that is what the words mean it was primarily due to that home that the boy became so sensitive to inward promptings and divine leadings. Good old "righteous Christer" did much by his rugged life and example to make the youth "pure and righteous," faithful inwardly to God and outwardly to man, saying even while a boy only "yea" and "nay," with no word in his vocabulary stronger than "verily"—"my words few and savoury, seasoned with grace." We see here, of course, in this family the ripened puritan ideals and the interior depth which characterized that movement at its best in the middle-class homes of the country.

This "yea" and "nay" of Fox deserves more than a passing mention. It was a fundamental characteristic not only of the boy, but of the man throughout all the stress and strain of his busy years. He was direct and straightforward. There were no worming ways, no eeling twists and turns in his nature. He looked a hard, stern alternative calmly in the face and said "yes" to it when he heard its challenge in his soul. There was something more, however, than *directness* behind his "yea" and "nay." It was his quality of native simplicity and sincerity. Nearly all his life long, costly peculiarities were at bottom due to this deep-lying trait. He wanted to *seem* to be as he really *was*. He wanted the inside view which lay open to God to be exactly like the outside view which was there for human observation. Hypocrisy, duplicity, sham appeared to him to be among the most heinous sins. He must not say "good morning," or "your humble servant," unless in the depths of his soul he intended those words to stand for an attitude of reality. He was resolved to live in the severe limits of "yes" and "no" until he saw something more that he could honestly say. His fine phrase, "Be what ye speak," expresses his deepest purpose.

There is at the early stage of Fox's development no possibility of tracing the influence of the parish church upon him. When he was about fourteen years old Nathaniel Stephens came to Drayton as curate and the effect of his ministry, a negative effect, is, at a later time, almost certainly in evidence, but there is no way of recovering the character of the teaching and preaching in the Drayton church during the period before Stephens' arrival on the scene. It can be safely assumed that the English Bible, read at home, was in any case in these early years a far stronger influence than were the sermons which he heard or the service in which he joined. It is cause for regret that the marvellous quality of the English Bible did not work a similar miraculous transformation in Fox's style of writing as was produced in the case of his famous contemporary in Bedford, John Bunyan, who had a corresponding lack of systematic education and a less favourable environment.

At some unknown youthful date, the boy was apprenticed, or "put," as he says, "to a man who was a shoemaker by trade." This brief connection with shoemaking gave Carlyle the basis for his famous picture of Fox as "he spreads out his cutting-board for the last time and cuts cowhides by unwonted patterns, and stitches them together into one continuous all-including case [his suit of leather], the farewell service of his awl! Stitch away, thou noble Fox: every prick of that little instrument is pricking into the heart of Slavery, and World-worship and the Mammon-god. Thy elbows jerk, in strong swimmer strokes, and every stroke is bearing thee across the Prison ditch, within which Vanity holds her Work-house and Rag-

fair, into lands of true Liberty; were the work
done, there is in broad Europe one free man
and thou art he!" [1]

The picture is of course quite imaginary, for
leather suits, especially leather breeches, were
very common and easily purchasable during
the period of the Civil War, when Fox donned
his suit for practical reasons. Croese, the Dutch
biographer of Fox, says that the shoemaker to
whom he was "put" lived in Nottingham. He
was a sheep and cattle grazer as well as a shoemaker, and he did an extensive business in wool.
William Penn says that Fox took delight in
sheep and was very skilful with them. It was,
Penn adds, "an employment that very well
suited his mind in several respects both from
its innocency and solitude." But Fox's own account implies that he managed the business in
an office rather than the sheep in a solitary pas-
ture. "A great deal [of business] went through
my hands," the *Journal* says, "and after I left
him [the employer], he broke and came to
nothing." [2]

There is no indication in Fox's life, up to
his nineteenth year, of any abnormal traits, or
of any unusual nervous strain. The one unique

[1] *Sartor Resartus*, b. iii, ch. i.   [2] *Journal*, p. 2.

characteristic about him was the fact that he was more free from taint of evil and less hampered by the appeal of a lower nature than the common run of boys. He seems to have been what William James called "a once-born soul," living spontaneously in purity and righteousness, as though that were a normal feature of life. There is no sign during these years of his youth that the Calvinistic conception of human nature as fundamentally ruined and totally depraved had made any impression on his mind. He tells us that from childhood he had learned how to use all created things of the world to the glory of Him who created them.[1] He reflects the joy of life and the naïve wonder which are such a striking feature of life in the pages of Thomas Traherne, who was born a decade later than was Fox and who wrote:

How like an angel came I down!
　How bright are all things here!
　When first among His works I did appear
O how their glory me did crown!
The world resembled His *Eternity*
　In which my soul did walk;
And everything that I did see
　Did with me talk.[2]

[1] *Journal*, p. 1.　　[2] Traherne's poem, "Wonder."

[14]

We are now to see this Drayton youth, once so free and guileless, suddenly plunged into a pitiful depression, and we shall be called to follow this "once-born soul" as he travels through bottomless deeps of agony and long onsets of temptation. The crisis came in 1643, during the period of the Civil War, when he was nineteen years old. The trivial nature of the occasion and the intensity of the shock and up-heaval plainly indicate that there was a hidden emotional force which surged up within him from below his threshold of consciousness.

His own account of the event is as follows:[3] "When I came towards nineteen years of age, being upon business at a fair, one of my cousins, whose name was Bradford, having another pro-fessor [4] with him, came and asked me to drink part of a jug of beer with them. I, being thirsty, went in with them.

"When we had drunk a glass apiece, they began to drink healths, and called for more drink, agreeing together that he that would not drink should pay all. I was grieved that any who made

[3] *Journal*, p. 3.

[4] "Professor" means here a nominal Christian. Our modern substitute for the expression would be "a church member."

profession of religion should offer to do so. They grieved me very much, having never had such a thing put to me before by any sort of people. Wherefore I rose up, and, putting my hand in my pocket, took out a groat, and laid it upon the table before them, saying, 'If it be so, I will leave you.'

"So I went away; and when I had done my business returned home; but did not go to bed that night, nor could I sleep, but sometimes walked up and down, and sometimes prayed and cried to the Lord, who said unto me: 'Thou seest how young people go together into vanity, and old people into the earth; thou must forsake all, young and old, keep out of all, and be as a stranger unto all.'

"Then, at the command of God, the ninth of the Seventh month, 1643, I left my relations, and broke off all familiarity or fellowship with young or old."

There is here no indication of moral struggle and no sense of temptation on his own part to do wrong. The thing that threw him into commotion was the discovery that professions of religion were hollow in the lives of those who composed the Church. The incident was trivial, but it was sufficient to reveal the fact that theological phrases had no practical bearing on life and that professions of Christianity for church purposes were empty and futile in the sphere of action. His commotion and agony were due to the sudden flash of discovery, after long repression of the unwelcome fact, that Christianity as interpreted in the theological preaching from church pulpits was in seventeenth-century England a dead and ineffective affair. His conclusion obviously rested on a very slender basis of evidence. It came from an emotional burst rather than from a rational demonstration, but for him it carried all the force of a divine revelation, coupled with a command to break completely with existent organised Christianity and to become a lonely seeker.

It seems probable that the extreme theology of Nathaniel Stephens, first curate and then rector of the Drayton church, was one of the psychological factors behind his emotional state. Stephens' appalling pictures of man's fall and depravity, of Satan's dominion over the world and over man's life, and his harrowing accounts of eternal torment for all who were non-elect must have profoundly affected this sensitive youth who had apparently grown up under a wholly different conception of the world and of human life. It is very probable, furthermore, that he had already in Nottingham or elsewhere come into contact with the fresh and dynamic ideas of the freer spiritual movements which were abroad. The contact may have been either with individual interpreters or through the little books and tracts which were already in wide circulation. The essential aspects of these freer spiritual movements were the proclamation of *a religion of life* and a faith in the divine possibilities of man's nature.

In any case, the break with the Drayton church and its theology was complete and final, and this young man of nineteen, tender, sensitive, pure-minded, but thrown into profound revolt, set forth on a passionate quest for truth and reality, and especially to find somewhere in England a type of religion which went beyond words and phrases and emerged with power in life and action. We need not follow his wanderings in detail. His own account supplies extremely little significant material. His conviction that theological preachers were hollow and spiritually useless was greatly increased by his interviews with them. They revealed themselves to him to be blind guides and empty cisterns—"empty, hollow casks," is his vivid phrase. They had no vital word "to speak to his condition." He was no doubt everywhere on the watch for clues of life and intimation of truth from persons who belonged to the freer spiritual movements of the time, especially the Seekers, the Anabaptists, and the Family of Love. Unfortunately, he gives us extremely few glimpses that throw any light on his path. There is no reference to any books which he read except the Bible and there are no reports of effective contacts. In London he visited his "uncle Pickering," who was a Baptist. He found the Baptists "tender," but he could not feel free to join them.

The accounts in the *Journal* have much to say of the "temptations" which beset him at this stage of his life, but they are almost certainly not what we usually understand by "temptations." They move for the most part in the sphere of the mind. They are temptations to doubt the great realities of religion, or to give up his pursuit of truth, or to accept some lower substitute for the highest, or they are questionings within himself as to whether he had done right to break with the church and to leave his home folks. With the doubts and temptations came also a profound depression and states of inward agony which shook his frame and threatened his health and sanity.

The symptoms and the reactions in the case of Fox are quite similar to those that appeared in the crisis-period of the life of St. Francis of Assisi. The emotional strain involved in the uncertainty of the path of life, in the seriousness of a momentous break with all existing habits of thought and conventions of life, worked unconsciously within him pretty much the way "shell shock" does, and played havoc with the physical system. The expert in these matters finds plenty of evidence in the cases of both St. Francis and George Fox of nervous instability and of abnormal symptoms such as tendency to temporary blindness, muscular control of the blood, prolonged trance-states, and consciousness of voices or of sights when no external object was present. In both cases a great spiritual experience brought reintegration of personality with an immense increase of energy and power, together with the illuminating discovery of the path of life and a fresh message for the age.

George Fox's constructive experience came at the end of three years of alternate wandering and eager quest in his home at Drayton. It was a characteristic mystical experience. The years of search which had seemed so empty of result had all the time been cumulatively fruit-ful in preparing him unconsciously for the spiritual intuitions which now broke into his soul. He had been slowly coming to see that Christ is not a dead Christ but a living One, that His vital work for man's salvation did not terminate on the Cross, but that He is operat-ing continuously as a real presence in the world, and that all spiritual processes have their sphere within the soul of man and not outside in "sa-cred" places. What Fox calls an "opening" was a flash of insight which suddenly brought to clear consciousness in him a truth which had lain latent and which henceforth became a prac-tical driving principle in his life.

Here is his own interesting account of his creative mystical experience:[1]

"When all my hopes in them [that is, in priests] and in all men were gone, so that I had nothing outwardly to help me, nor could I tell what to do, then, oh, then, I heard a voice which said, 'There is one, even Christ Jesus, that can speak to thy condition'; and when I heard it my heart did leap for joy. Thus when God doth work, who shall hinder it? and this

[1] *Journal*, pp. 11-12.

I knew experimentally. My desire after the Lord grew stronger, and zeal in the pure knowledge of God, and of Christ alone, without the help of any man, book, or writing. For though I read the Scriptures that spoke of Christ and of God, yet I knew Him not, but by revelation, as He who hath the key did open, and as the Father of Life drew me to His Son by His Spirit. Then the Lord gently led me along, and let me see His love, which was endless and eternal, surpassing all the knowledge that men have in the natural state, or can obtain from history or books; and that love let me see myself, as I was without Him."

CHAPTER III

Fox as a New Type of Mystic

I'll build all inward—not a light shall ope
The common out-way.—
I'll therefore live in dark; and all my light,
Like ancient temples, let in at my top.
                    —GEORGE CHAPMAN.

THE "new psychologists" divide men into two classes, those who are called "introverts," and those who are called "extroverts" —the "in-lookers," or "in-turners," and the "out-lookers," or "out-turners." George Fox was both "introvert" and "extrovert" in about equal degree. Josiah Royce, who made a careful psychological study of him a quarter of a century before this new jargon was invented, found Fox to be a man who was essentially keyed for action. His focus of attention, Professor Royce maintains, was toward movement, action, deed. He was a traveller, an organiser, a doer. His disposition was that of a person whose will-purpose rose above his reflective powers. Fox would have agreed with his contemporary, Gerrard Winstanley, who wrote: "My mind was not at rest, because nothing was acted; and thoughts ran in me that words and writings were nothing and must die; for action is the life of all, and *if thou dost not act thou dost nothing*." [1]

This emphasis on action which Josiah Royce discovered as a central trait of Fox's character is undoubtedly a sound diagnosis and it can be verified by any reader of the *Journal*, but it is only half of the truth. There was a stage in his life when he was *preparing* for action rather than acting, when, to quote George Chapman's line, he was "building all inward" and storing up an immense reservoir of energies for those years of stress and strain during which he was to move about the world as an irresistible leader of a dynamic movement.

The word "mystic" is capable of almost endless interpretations, but many expert writers would contend that, with all its width of reach, it does not properly apply to George Fox. The

[1] *A Watchword to the City of London* (1649), Dedicatory Letter.

mystic of history, these experts maintain, is a person who by an undeviating *via negativa,* or way of negation, climbs the lonely ladder of purgation, illumination, and union, attaining at the top of the steep and rugged ascent an ineffable and ecstatic state of absorption into the absolute Godhead. This pathway upward, "the mystic way" of the great exponents of contemplation, is essentially a type of Roman Catholic piety, and it is always taken for granted by the sympathetic interpreters of it that the exalted experience is supernaturally initiated and is therefore a special work of divine grace in the soul. It involves a stern withdrawal from the world, from outward helps, from processes of thinking and reasoning, from symbols and images, and calls for a miraculous leap or flight from the things that are in time to *That Which Eternally Is.* From the nature of the case the mystical experience of this negative type is unutterable, and incapable of interpretation in terms of anything we know or see. It remains forever something apart, something wholly unique and *sui generis.*

If mysticism is to be confined to that one fixed type, then quite certainly George Fox was not a "mystic." He had no well-defined "mystic way." He did not believe that it was necessary "to go anywhere," up a mystic ladder or down a devious stairway, to find God. God and man for him were so near to each other that no "distance" at all intervened. The real discovery for him was the essential fact of life that there is something of God in man as man. A precious immortal seed of God is hidden in man's soul, and the supreme moment of life is that moment when one awakens to the fact that this heavenly Godlike reality is in us and can expand and become our true complete life. Fox's mysticism is not of a negative type; it is essentially affirmative. His highest moments are not ecstatic and ineffable. They are moments when his inner life feels flooded or invaded by the real presence which is always there, but which only occasionally surges up into consciousness. Instead of terminating his quest with an abstract Absolute, he always insists on the concrete character of God, as being like Christ, as tender and loving, as a warm and intimate Companion and Friend. His tremendous assertion is that he knows God *experimentally*. "I was as one who had a key and did open."

There appear to have been two or three years in the formative period of Fox's life, perhaps from 1645 to 1648, when this work of "building all inward," of finding his sense of direction, and of accumulating that mighty conviction, was the most important feature of his life. He was always an affirmation mystic, but these years before he had an impressive following and was carried into the turmoil of a busy life are the years during which his mystical experiences are most intense and most frequent. Before he had the typical constructive experience which was reported at the end of the last chapter, he had already discovered that the only true temple where God reveals Himself is in the human heart. Men and women are temples, revealing places for God, while structures made of stone and mortar can never be revealing places; and the priestly "anointing" which brings spiritual illumination and wisdom to the soul is a divine anointing by the chrism of the Spirit within man.[1] After the great experience had turned him from despair to triumphant joy he moved steadily forward in his discovery of the divine revealed within him. I knew God and Christ now, he says, not through books and Scriptures, but *by revelation*, as he who hath the key did open and as the Father of Life drew me to His

[1] *Journal*, p. 8.

Son by His Spirit. The Lord gently led me along and let me see His love, which was endless and eternal . . . and that love let me see myself, as I was without Him.[1]

Fox admits throughout his account that he diligently read and loved the Bible; in fact, he almost knew it by heart, but he was quite unaware of the extent to which he owed his discoveries to it and even more unaware how much he owed to the spiritual dissenters with whom he came in contact on his travels. Christ, he says again and again, *opened* the door of Light and Life to me. My inward mind was joined to His Seed and thus inward life sprang up in me. I saw the great love of God and I was filled with admiration at the infinitude of it. I was wrapt up in the love of God so that I could not but admire the greatness of His love.[2] All this spiritual process and progress seemed to the young enthusiastic mystic to spring wholly from within him and to be entirely an inward revelation. He leaped to the conclusion that the divine revealing and saving work which is progressively going on in man's soul has no known limits or terminus. The goal is a perfect, completely redeemed and transformed life.

[1] *Journal*, p. 12, quoted freely.   [2] *Journal*, pp. 12-14.

It seems pretty evident that Fox was strongly influenced in his conception of salvation by the Familists, a widespread mystical sect of the period. They owed their origin and their body of ideas to a Dutch mystic named Henry Nicholas (born 1501). The substance of his teaching was an insistence on the possibility of a complete conquest over sin and of an attainment of a new and transformed nature which is victorious over the impulses of the flesh. His complaint against the Church was that it expected its members to remain "miserable sinners," and did not proclaim a type of godliness in which sin is conquered or destroyed. He attacked what he considered the fiction of "imputed" righteousness and forensic, or legal, holiness, and called instead for the attainment of *real righteousness and of actual holiness of life.* The true goal of life, in his view, was a state of character in which Christ is *formed* in the man so that he becomes a triumphant soul.

That is exactly Fox's position. His long depression had been due not to his own personal battle with sin, but rather to his discovery that church members and professing Christians of the time lived, in the main, like other people and had no mark of victory in their lives. Christianity seemed to be ineffective and abortive. His own great experience of an inward resident power strengthened and confirmed his faith that salvation must be proclaimed as first of all a way of victory over sin. This was a primary note in his message.

"Salvation" is for Fox complete normal spiritual health and moral power—a victorious life. The incorruptible seed of God, he stoutly maintained, can produce, and ought to produce, a full-grown, holy, and sinless life. That exalted claim which Fox made at the outset of his ministry threw all the "professors," he says, "into a rage," for they all "pleaded for sin and imperfection." "None of them could bear to be told that any should come to Adam's perfection, into the image of God." He was asked at Derby in 1649 whether he was "sanctified," "and," he says, "I answered, yes; for I was in the paradise of God. Then they asked me, If I had no sin? I answered 'Christ, my Saviour, has taken away my sin, and in Him is no sin.' " [1]

There is obviously in this view of life a complete break with the Calvinistic conception of man. However little Fox suspected it, he was essentially a "humanist," in the noble sense of

[1] *Journal*, pp. 50-51.

the word, in his estimate of man's nature and of man's immense possibilities. The spiritual reformers of the sixteenth century were as much influenced by the humanism of Erasmus as they were by the spiritual messages of the mystics, and that strong, wholesome, optimistic outlook of humanism had, without his knowing how he came by it, become an inherent part of the mental climate of Fox.

We have seen that it was one of the peculiar traits of Fox's character that latent ideas, more or less unconsciously formed attitudes, suddenly surged up and became a live and dynamic *experience*, with immense driving power. One of his most remarkable experiences of this sort had to do with this attitude of his toward the formation of the new victorious inward nature. The *idea* was not new. It lay at the heart of the teaching of the Familists, and it was a central view of Jacob Boehme's mysticism which was beginning to circulate in England when Fox began his wanderings. Some time in 1647 or 1648 occurred the experience to which I have referred and which Fox has described at a later period in language that is deeply coloured by Jacob Boehme's phrases.

"Now I was come up in spirit through the

flaming sword, into the paradise of God. All things were new; and all the creation gave unto me another smell than before, beyond what words can utter. I knew nothing but pureness, and innocency, and righteousness; being renewed into the image of God by Christ Jesus, to the state of Adam, which he was in before he fell. The creation was opened to me; and it was showed me how all things had their names given them according to their nature and virtue.

"I was at a standstill in my mind whether I should practise physic for the good of mankind, seeing the nature and virtues of things were so opened to me by the Lord. But I was immediately taken up in spirit to see into another or more steadfast state than Adam's innocency, even into a state in Christ Jesus that should never fall. And the Lord showed me that such as were faithful to Him, in the power and light of Christ, should come up into that state in which Adam was before he fell; in which the admirable works of the creation, and the virtues thereof, may be known, through the openings of that divine Word of wisdom and power by which they were made.

"Great things did the Lord lead me into, and wonderful depths were opened unto me, beyond what can by words be declared; but as people come into subjection to the Spirit of God, and grow up in the image and power of the Almighty, they may receive *the Word of wisdom that opens all things, and come to know the hidden unity in the Eternal Being.*" [1]

Here is something more than *ideas* intellectually accepted. The flaming sword and the paradise of God are no longer pictorial figures in a book; they have become realities of life, tested and verified in a personal experience. The imagery employed in the account was an inheritance from the mystics on the continent and had been vividly used, as I have said, in the writings of Boehme. "The flaming sword," which symbolized man's fall and expulsion from fellowship with God, is now superseded by the triumphant work of the Spirit in man's soul, and by the Spirit he can come back, not only to the state of Adam's original innocency, but to the higher stage of the formation of a permanent Christ-nature within. "And," says Fox, "I have myself come into that experience!" The "new smell" may be either "the smell of the lily," which in Boehme and other mystics symbolised the new era of the

1 *Journal*, pp. 28-29.

[33]

Spirit, or it may be a kind of fore-smell of the actual paradise flowers! [1]

Fox had many other mystical experiences through which his convictions were raised to mighty forces of life and his dim gropings for light became clear "openings" of truth. "I saw the divine light of Christ shine through all," he says, "and I had pure openings of the light without the help of any man." As he was walking in the fields one day, there surged up into his consciousness the words which seemed to come from God himself, saying, "Thy name is written in the Lamb's book of Life which was before the foundation of the world, and I saw in this the new birth." Another time a tender voice seemed to say in his soul, "My love was always to thee and thou art in my love." It was through such experiences that his inward man was built. [2]

The most beautiful of all his mystical "openings" was one that came to him in 1647, probably before he had begun his mission of

[1] A passage in Fox's *Epistle CCXXXV* inclines me to think that he has the smell of the lily in mind. He says in his *Epistle*, "And so think not the winter and cold weather, nor the night, long; for *the lilies do grow and the gardens do give a good smell.*"

[2] *Journal*, pp. 35 and 47.

preaching. "I saw," he said, "that there was an ocean of darkness and death; but an infinite ocean of light and love, which flowed over the ocean of darkness. In that I saw the infinite love of God." [1]

Here we have a characteristic trait of what I have called Fox's "affirmation mysticism." His experiences always lead up not to a vague blank or to an ineffable contact with an Absolute, but to a vivified consciousness of the concrete and definite character of God. Fox belongs in a class with persons like Socrates and Joan of Arc and Samuel Taylor Coleridge, who possessed a peculiar mental constitution which enabled them to draw upon their deeper submerged life and to attain by flashes and intuitions a profounder wisdom and an acuter conviction of reality than they could arrive at by processes of *thinking*. Coleridge's poems, "The Ancient Mariner" and "Kubla Khan," are almost entirely made out of the survivals and detritus from his readings of books of travel and description. They came back, however, not as broken scraps and disintegrated ashes, but as fused, organised, harmonised, beautified, melodious re-creations. Somewhere within the

[1] See *Journal*, pp. 19-20.

deeper levels of the poet's mind the forging processes had gone on and the poet in his creative moments builded better than he knew, giving back the latent material in immortal forms of beauty. So, too, the wisdom of Socrates and the insight of the Maid of Orleans were in scope and range far beyond their conscious thought or their capacity to prove. They *arrived* by a way which they knew not.

George Fox was distinctly of that type—the type of the prophet and the creative genius. His openings, his flashes of insight, his truths, do not need to be called miraculous communications or supernatural interventions, but they do presuppose a peculiar capacity of nature to mature and ripen ideas and principles of life below the level of thought and to have them surge up, fused with emotional heat and interpenetrated with a sense of a divine origin. Such was his nature, and he was sent on his mission by impelling convictions, which seemed to have their sphere of birth beyond the margin of his own mind.

All the mystics of this type are impressed with the feeling and live on the basic assumption that God is within and not beyond. They think of their inner selves as resting upon the deeper

Life of the Spirit that is always within call and hail. Intimations of light and guidance, upwellings of life and wisdom, seem to be "given," and the love of God seems to flow around their incompleteness and bring to them peace and power. May it not, in fact, be so? Is it not possible that God is a Beyond within us and that the spiritual nature in us partakes of and is kin to the Eternal Spirit who is the true environment of our finite spirits?

Fox did not try to think out or to formulate any such interpretation of life, but he felt surrounded and invaded, and he was sure that light and life and love and truth from beyond himself lay suddenly at hand for his use. This "inward-building" is what prepared him for an outward practical mission.

CHAPTER IV

Getting the Movement Under Way

IT IS well-nigh impossible to fix with final certainty the date at which George Fox began his itinerant mission of interpretation to the world. In his introductory preface to his published *Epistles,* he declares that "the truth sprang up first to us to be a people of the Lord, in Leicestershire in 1644, and in Warwickshire in 1645, and in Nottinghamshire in 1646, and in Derbyshire in 1647." It is quite certain that he is led here in retrospect to put the dates too early. It may be, of course, that in the early years of his quest for light he came upon persons, or even small bands, here and there in the counties, who later joined him and helped to form the nucleus of the local Quaker groups. But there is no available indication of any proclamation of his message, nor any evidence of "convincements" to his truth before the year 1647. He says in the *Journal,* in his brief account of a visit to Dukinfield and Manchester: "I declared truth among them [the professors] and there were some convinced, who received the Lord's teaching, by which they were confirmed and stood in the truth." [1] That is the first sure testimony at hand for the beginning of Fox's public ministry. There are no names given of any persons "convinced," though we have here for the first time the well-known phrase used, "The Lord's power was over all." A little later his "mouth was opened and the everlasting truth was declared" at a great meeting of the Baptists held at Broughton. Both of these occasions were in 1647.

A tiny spark of light is thrown into the darkness, which pretty well covers the early period of his mission, by a reference in John Whiting's *Persecution Exposed*, which indicates that Fox was "travelling up and down, and working at his Trade (which was that of a Shoemaker) between whiles, particularly at Mansfield in Nottinghamshire, till about the year 1647. He began more particularly [then] to declare the Truth as he had received it in Christ Jesus freely to others." [2]

[1] *Journal*, p. 18.
[2] Whiting, *Persecution Exposed* (1715), p. 208.

It may be just possible that his original apprenticeship was here, in or near Mansfield. We have seen that Croese, the Dutch biographer of Fox, who wrote the earliest Life of him, made the unconditioned statement that George as a youth was "put out" to a man in Nottingham, which may no doubt mean in the county rather than in the town of Nottingham. Nottinghamshire was well supplied with persons of the dissenter class and Fox undoubtedly later made some of his first "convincements" in that part of the country. The passage already quoted from John Whiting's memoirs is conclusive evidence that Fox was working at his trade of shoemaker as he travelled up and down the country in the seeker years, 1643-47.

There is a puzzling passage in William Rogers's *Christian-Quaker* [1] which says: "Before he [Fox] went abroad to preach the Light, [*i.e.*, before 1647] he was a Journey Man Shoemaker and as such an one wrought Journey work with George Gee of Manchester." That does not, I am convinced, refer to his original apprenticeship, but rather to a later period of temporary work as a journeyman. Rogers's statement fits in well with a passage already quoted describing

[1] *The Christian-Quaker* (1680), Part V, p. 48.

Fox's movements at or near the end of his period of quest [*i.e.*, about 1647]. "Passing on," he says, "I went among the 'professors' at Dukinfield and Manchester where I stayed awhile." [1] It may very well have been at this time when he "stayed awhile" at Manchester that he worked with the aforesaid George Gee, of whom we know nothing further.

From Manchester he went to Mansfield, as the *Journal* plainly shows, at which place he made a considerable sojourn, and this period of sojourn in Mansfield is confirmed by John Whiting, who says that he was working at his shoemaker trade as he travelled, "particularly at Mansfield in Nottinghamshire about the year 1647." I assume that he was now back once more in or near the region where he had lived as an apprentice and where he knew persons who were in sympathy with his type of thought, as the context of the *Journal* indicates.

There is finally a significant passage in a book by Henry Pickworth,[2] which tells us, on the indefinite authority of George Keith, that George Fox was "originally taught" his doc-

[1] *Journal*, p. 18.
[2] *A Short Account of the People Called Quakers, Showing Their Deceitful Ways* (1735), p. 17.

[41]

trines "by one Hinks, a Ranter, whilst they kept sheep together" (p. 17), presumably in Nottinghamshire. The word "Ranter" need not be taken too seriously here. It was used in the seventeenth century much as the word "Bolshevist" has been used by conservative persons in our time, to characterise anyone who is inclined to deviate from settled and established lines of thought or practice. "Seekers" were often loosely called "Ranters," and so, too, were "Familists" and "Anabaptists." We know nothing further of this man Hinks, but Fox may very likely have been thrown at this time of apprenticeship with a person of unsettled and unsettling views.[1]

In any case, his first extensive missionary labours appear to have been in Nottinghamshire, centering around Mansfield and Nottingham, where he seems to be in intimate contact with a large number of "separatists" of different types, whom he may very well have known in the former period of his shoemaking apprenticeship. He says of the outlook at this opening period of his ministry: "I saw the harvest white and the seed of God lying thick in the ground,

[1] I suspect that he was Richard Hinks, who later became a radical, dissenting preacher.

as ever did wheat that was sown outwardly.
. . . The Lord's power broke forth and I had
great openings and prophecies."[1] On one occasion at a great meeting, apparently of "separatists" at Mansfield, Fox was moved to offer
prayer, and he remarks, "the Lord's power was
so great that the house seemed to be shaken."[2]
Many years later William Penn said of Fox:
"Above all he excelled in prayer. The most
awful, living, reverent frame I ever felt or be-
held, I must say, was his in prayer."[3]

At the very beginning of his labours among
these spiritual "separatists" in Nottinghamshire,
Fox had "convinced" a remarkable woman
named Elizabeth Hooton that he himself had
found what they as separatists were all seeking.
"She was," he says, "a very tender woman,"
which meant for him spiritually-minded and
solidly religious. She became the first public
propagator of the message which Fox was in-
terpreting, and she proved to be a strong helper,
as she was also a great sufferer for her faith
throughout her long and valiant life.

Another prominent convert in this early Nottinghamshire period was Amor Stoddard, who

[1] *Journal*, p. 21.   [2] *Ibid.*, p. 24.
[3] Preface to *Journal*, p. *xlvii.*

[43]

was a captain in Cromwell's army, and who from this time until his death was a noble helper and companion to George Fox. When "the professors" at Mansfield endeavoured to bear Fox down with words, and to stop him from speaking, Captain Stoddard "was reached" by the bearing of the brave young man and said to the crowd with authority, "Let the youth speak; hear the youth speak." When Amor Stoddard was dying in 1670, George Fox visited him and was moved to say to the dying man, "Thou hast been faithful as a man, and faithful to God; and the immortal seed of life is thy crown." [1]

So far as appears, this Nottinghamshire group of spiritual "separatists" forms the first real body of followers whom Fox secured, though Nottinghamshire and Leicestershire should perhaps be linked together. It was here that the delightful name of "Children of the Light" was adopted as the name for those who joined the new movement. The name was peculiarly appropriate for a people whose central faith was in the Light of Christ as it was revealed within themselves. Gradually another name, that of "Friends" or "Friends in the Truth," sup-

[1] *Journal*, ii, p. 132.

planted the early name Children of the Light, but we have here, I think, the genuine birthplace and the first setting of the Quaker movement. Here, as everywhere during the lifetime of Fox, the members who formed the new movement were of the separatist-seeker type and not members of the established Church. Fox, as he looked back to this early stage, made this significant entry in his *Journal*: "The Lord's power was wonderfully manifested both at Mansfield and other neighboring towns." [1]

It is probable that shoemaking and preaching went on alternately, with headquarters at Mansfield for a good part of the time during the years 1647-49, though there were occasional journeys farther afield. The first public challenge to the old system which was given in a church occurred at Nottingham in the early part of 1649, the first year of the Commonwealth. Fox was on his way, one Sunday morning, to a meeting with the Children of the Light, to whom, when he wrote his *Journal*, he already applied the name "Friends," [2] when his eye caught sight of the "steeplehouse" of the town, and he instantly felt that he heard a voice within say, "Thou must go cry against yonder

[1] *Journal*, p. 27.   [2] *Ibid.*, 42.

great idol and against the worshippers therein."
The old complex against the Church system and
its forms of worship is as strong in him as ever,
and his emotional conflict with all the signs and
symbols of these forms surges up as hot and
intense as ever. He went on to the meeting,
"where the power of the Lord was mighty
amongst us," and then the young prophet went
forth to bear his testimony against "yon great
idol." His own account of the scene which follows is vivid and is very revealing as to his state
of mind:

"He [the Nottingham minister] took for
his text these words of Peter, 'We have also a
more sure Word of prophecy, whereunto ye
do well that ye take heed, as unto a light that
shineth in a dark place, until the day dawn,
and the day-star arise in your hearts.' And he
told the people that this was the Scriptures, by
which they were to try all doctrines, religions,
and opinions.

"Now the Lord's power was so mighty upon
me, and so strong in me, that I could not hold,
but was made to cry out and say, 'Oh, no; it
is not the Scriptures!' and I told them what
it was, namely, the Holy Spirit, by which the
holy men of God gave forth the Scriptures,

whereby opinions, religions, and judgments were to be tried; for it led into all truth, and so gave knowledge of all truth. The Jews had the Scriptures and yet resisted the Holy Ghost, and rejected Christ, the bright morning star. They persecuted Christ, and His apostles and took upon them to try their doctrines by the Scriptures; but they erred in judgment, and did not try them aright, because they tried without the Holy Ghost.

"But that day the Lord's power sounded so in their ears that they were amazed at the voice, and could not get it out of their ears for some time after, they were so reached by the Lord's power in the steeplehouse." [1]

The interruption of a sermon was illegal and this is the only time that Fox impulsively broke in without permission on a legitimate service. His emotion and his sense of divine impulsion overcame him and he had to take the natural consequences of his act. "The officers came," he says in the *Journal*, "and took me away and put me in a nasty, stinking prison"—the first of his many prison experiences. It was of short duration, for at the assizes he was released without further ado. His jailer was "convinced" and

[1] *Journal*, pp. 42-43.

became a Child of the Light, and some un-
named person came up to the assizes and offered
himself body for body as a substitute sufferer
for Fox.

The challenge to the minister in Nottingham
reveals very effectively the substance of the
message which Fox was proclaiming at this
period of his preaching. The coming of the day-
dawn and the rising of the day-star in the soul
is the word of which he is the herald. He is
forward-looking, not backward-looking. It is
not an event of ancient history that concerns
him; it is an event in the human heart to which
he calls men. The Christ who was born in
Bethlehem is still coming to birth in man and
the star is no longer far away in the sky in the
East; it rises with its heavenly Light in the
soul and makes the whole life radiant with its
shining. It seemed worth while to interrupt the
dull hour-glass sermon with a fresh word like
that. Fox says with naïve simplicity, "The
Lord's power so sounded in their ears that day,
that they could not get it out of their ears for
some time after, they were so reached by the
Lord's power in the steeplehouse." [1]

I shall pass rapidly over the events of the

[1] *Journal*, p. 43.

next two years (1650-52), one whole year of the period having been spent by Fox in Derby jail. He had gone to the "steeplehouse" of the town, where, as he was allowed by law to do, he spoke after the minister had finished his sermon. Officers came and hailed him before the magistrates. He used the opportunity for expounding his spiritual conception of religion, telling those who gathered in throngs to see him that they should stop *disputing* about Christ and instead *obey* Him. He was committed to prison for six months under the act against blasphemy. A great many visitors came to see him and to discuss the issues of life with him in the prison. The jailer was converted, as often happened with Fox's keepers.

It was at this time that Justice Bennett fixed the name of "Quaker" upon Fox and his movement. Fox implies in his account that the name was due to the fact that he bade the judge tremble, that is, *quake,* before the Lord, but the real reason that the name stuck and became permanent was that the Children of the Light undoubtedly trembled in their meetings with emotional fervour and there were times when a wave of tremulous quaking would suddenly sweep over the entire group. There is, too, plenty of evidence to indicate that individual Friends sometimes had attacks of involuntary and uncontrollable *quaking*, so that even without the episode in the Magistrate's court the name "Quaker" was a natural sobriquet for the new movement, and the word was in actual fact already coined as a religious nickname before the Derby application was made and before Fox began his mission. One of the most characteristic incidents of the imprisonment was an attempt which was made to get rid of the prisoner without further legal machinery, by giving him permission to walk a mile for exercise. Fox refused to take advantage of the permission unless the authorities would first measure off an exact mile!

He wrote many documents during his confinement, but, alas! he did not possess the miraculous quality of style which could lift his words into immortal power, as was the case a little later with another prisoner, John Bunyan. An attempt was made at this time to commission him as captain in the army of the Commonwealth. This visit of the Commissioners gave Fox an occasion to formulate in noble fashion his way of life and his attitude toward war.[1] The position will be dealt with in due time. His term of imprisonment was eventually extended another six months after the first six months were completed and he was not released until the autumn of 1651. Soon after his release from prison occurred the famous episode in Lichfield, to which I shall refer in more detail in a later chapter.

While he was in the Derby jail he had almost certainly received information about the existence of a group of "separatists" in the neighbourhood of Doncaster in Yorkshire, which was only about ten miles from Scrooby, the original seat of the Congregational separatists who became the Pilgrim Fathers. The new groups of "separatists" scattered about in Yorkshire, of whom Fox had heard, were pretty definitely of the type known as "Seekers," whom I shall shortly describe, when Fox's travels bring him to the central region of the Seeker movement. It was in December 1651 that the young prophet, moving about on foot, came into his first contact with these Yorkshire separatists. Balby, Tickhill, Wakefield, and Warms-

[1] *Journal*, p. 68.

worth were some of the most active centres, and in these and other affected communities Fox made many "convincements" to his message and way of life. Some of his finest disciples and his most powerful helpers came out of these prepared groups. Wisest and best of them all was William Dewsbury, who later called his dungeons palaces and the bolts of his prison precious jewels. Out of these convincements of 1651 came James Nayler, a former quartermaster in the Parliamentary army, a great preacher and a great soul, notwithstanding the trouble he was one day to bring to the cause in which he enlisted. There were Thomas Aldam, Richard Farnsworth, Thomas Killam, and "honourable women not a few."

On this eventful journey he became acquainted with Justice Durant Hotham, who was one of the foremost English disciples of Jacob Boehme. Hotham had already proclaimed himself resolved to go forward "in the bed-route of those Seekers that walk unfettered in the quest of truth." He enthusiastically welcomed George Fox, and the latter calls him "a tender man who had some experience of God's workings in his heart." He took Fox in his arms after he had heard him speak and said, with real per-

sonal affection, "My house is from now on
your house." [1] Very different from the warmth
and fervour of Fox's reception among the Seekers was his treatment at the hands of the repre-
sentatives of the Church. He attempted to speak
in York Minster after the "priest" had finished
his service, but when he told the listeners that
God looked for fruits from their lives and not
pious words and notions, they hurried him out
of the Minster and threw him down the steps. [2]
Similar treatment came generally from those
who represented established religion and Fox
was often roughly handled by Yorkshire mobs.

We come now to the crisis and turning-point
of the new movement which Fox incarnated. In
Wensleydale and the marginal regions where
the three counties of Yorkshire, Lancashire and
Westmorland join together, and especially in
the neighbourhood of Sedbergh, there had existed for a long time in peaceful quiet isolation
large groups of Seekers. Their origin and early
history have not yet been authoritatively traced.
They were beyond question a direct fruit of

[1] I have given in my *Spiritual Reformers*, pp. 209-212,
the reasons for thinking that this Justice was Durant
Hotham.
[2] *Journal*, p. 84.

the seed which the spiritual reformers of the sixteenth century sowed. They were in spirit and manner of life like some of the small Mennonite groups in Holland and they had many points in common with the Dutch Collegiants with whom Spinoza lived for three years at Rynsburg.[1] But definite contacts between the English and continental groups have not yet been established. These Seekers in the northern counties had entirely severed connection with the established Churches. They had their own simple group organisation. They had monthly Meetings for the direction of their congregational affairs, which were held in the Chapel at Preston Patrick. They strongly emphasised the lay and democratic character of religion. It was to be a religion of life and spirit. They had discarded ordination. They believed that the sacraments of the Church lacked authority and efficacy. They discounted the importance of preaching and public prayer, though they did not wholly dispense with them. They had in their groups some powerful interpreters of their simple faith. But they exalted silence over words and they met together in the attitude of

[1] See my *Spiritual Reformers of the Sixteenth and Seventeenth Centuries*.

[54]

waiters and seekers, hoping and yearning that God in His own time would once more pour out His Spirit and baptise His waiting people with power and unction from on high, and would send among them some rightly equipped and divinely ordained apostle-prophet to inaugurate in their midst the new dispensation.

There was, consequently, a double search under way. George Fox had undoubtedly heard of them from his new friends about Balby and was on his way to find them, while they in their turn had for years been seeking for a new prophet, sent from God to lead them forward the next step into the fuller Light. Suddenly, like the contact of two electrodes, the new prophet and the Seeker groups met, with dynamic effect. It was like those divided souls about which Plato tells us in the *Symposium,* each half seeking its other half and finding fullness of life only in union.

There were interesting foregleams before the actual burst of light and joy came. Fox, with touching simplicity, has told us how he was prepared for what was to be the most important event in his ministry. He says, "As we travelled [Richard Farnsworth was his companion] we came near a very great hill, called Pendle Hill and I was moved of the Lord to go up to the top of it. . . . From the top of this hill the Lord let me see in what places he had a great people to be gathered." At the inn that evening, the vision from the hill-top was supplemented by a further sight of the coming event. "The Lord opened unto me," he says, "and let me see a great people in white raiment by a river side, coming to the Lord." [1] It took some time, in spite of the foresight and the guiding vision, to discover the people in white raiment waiting to be gathered, for not all the dwellers in these dales had the Seeker-attitude and not all of them were waiting for the other half of themselves to come. At length he came to Brigflatts on the River Rawthey, near Sedbergh, which flows near by into the River Lune, the County boundary, which was the place of his vision of a people in white raiment by a riverside. "White raiment" was a figure for spiritual preparation, and this quiet country district was on the edge of a wide-spreading and far-flung community of separated, seeking people, inwardly prepared for the message Fox was to bring them. They had given up what they felt were the dry, empty forms of the world's worship and the world's

[1] *Journal,* pp. 109-110.

religion and they were content to meet in silence and in hushed community prayer, while
they waited for the Spirit to qualify some one
of their members to speak or pray vocally for
the rest. This large group scattered through a
number of hamlets and rural sections of the
region met once a month, as I have said, for a
General Meeting at the Preston Patrick Chapel.
This was a few miles south of Kendal, where
some of the Seekers lived.

Fox had his first contact with this Seeker
group at a meeting in the home of a remarkable
man of the district named Gervase Benson. This
Benson home was at Borrat, a few miles up
the River Rawthey from Sedbergh, and here
a number of the Seekers were convinced by the
preaching of Fox. He followed up this good
beginning a little later "at a great Fair," where
he "declared the day of the Lord through the
Fair," that is, preaching as he moved about
among the people.

Then he went to "the steeple-house" yard
in Sedbergh and spoke for "several hours," setting forth in considerable fullness the substance
of his message, which I propose to interpret in
the next chapter. Francis Howgill, who was
one of the leading men of the Seekers and who

now heard Fox for the first time, announced confidently to the great throng that "this man speaks with authority and not as the Scribes." "Many people," the Journal says, "were convinced that day and were glad to hear the truth declared, and received it with joy." [1]

The real event of the visit, however, was the great Sunday meeting at the Firbank Chapel in Westmorland, on a lofty fellside, where there was a wide sweep of view. Francis Howgill and John Audland were present at the meeting in the morning and both spoke to the large separatist group that gathered for worship. Fox was walking about the yard, but did not feel ready to enter the meeting or to participate in it. But in the afternoon of that day he met the throng of about a thousand persons by appointment on the fellside above the chapel, taking his seat on a projecting rock, which still bears the name of "Fox's Pulpit." He was on the borderland of rapture during this meeting; a glow and radiance spread over his face and an unusual power attended his speaking, which went on for three wonderful hours. He apparently felt that "the hour had struck," "the day of the Lord had come!" Here the electrodes met and power

[1] *Journal*, p. 112.

was released. The Seekers recognised in Fox almost at once the apostolic man for whom they had been waiting, and he in turn found his "people in white raiment."

We do not need to follow in detail the busy days that succeeded, as the skilled fisher of men went from place to place, casting his net and pulling it in full of fishes. It was one of these men, Howgill himself, who said in this figure of the fishing: "The kingdom of God did gather us, and catch us all as in a net and His heavenly power at one time drew many hundreds to land."

This remarkable "convincement" of the Seekers in the northern counties is the true birth-occasion of the Society of Friends. There were great "convincements" to follow, but in the main they grew out of this first striking success of the new prophet. Out of this group came many of his most powerful helpers in the work of propagation, and from these people in white raiment he derived many of his ideas about organization and about worship.

Some of the noblest of his band of preachers who came out of the Seeker groups were: Francis Howgill, Edward Burrough, John Audland, John Camm, Richard Hubberthorne of

Yealand, Miles Halhead, Thomas Taylor, Jane and Dorothy Waugh, Ann Audland, Elizabeth Fletcher, and many more of lesser fame. There were soon to be no less than sixty men and women going forth with the net which until now Fox had, with meagre results, been casting alone.

CHAPTER V

Fox's Proclamation and Way of Life

WE MUST interrupt our story of Fox's travels in the northern counties to consider the message and interpretation of life which was being given by the "man in leather" who seemed to the Seekers to be a new prophet. The important point to emphasise is the fact that the message of Fox in the first instance came to those who heard it not as a cold, abstract theory, but rather as a principle of life embodied in a living character and made warm and intimate in terms of a concrete person who exhibited it in movement and practice and action. Fox himself was always protesting against what he called religious "notions." He felt a strong revulsion from the tendency to reduce religion to "phrases" or "statements" or "doctrinal formulations," for he saw with utmost clarity that they are wholly different from the true thing itself, which is, and must be, *an experience, a life, an incarnation,* if it is to be real and significant. We must, therefore, keep in mind throughout this chapter that any attempt to put the proclamation of this dynamic traveller over into an abstract phrase is to lose the throbbing, palpitating soul of it. It is like a visitor to the north, endeavouring to carry back a snowflake in his warm hand, to show it to the dwellers in the southland! It will not be a snowflake that he shows them when he arrives, but a mere drop of water!

It is customary to say that the central aspect of the message of Fox was the proclamation of an inward Light in man, but we must endeavour, if possible, to clothe that phrase with vitality and life and put it into its historical setting. The mystics of the fourteenth century had held the view that there is a divine apex in the soul of man which is essentially derived from God and which remains unlost and inalienable amid the ruin and wreckage of fallen nature. It is, according to these mystics, a point in common between God and man, a junction of the divine and human. No matter how far a man travels out into the finite and temporal, he yet never utterly breaks connection with his eternal Origin, but bears in the central substance of his being a link with the immortal Source of his birth. These fourteenth-century mystics often called this apex of the soul "the Spark," or "the Glimmer."

It was, however, Thomas Münzer, a radical reformer, a contemporary of Luther's, who first suggested the inward Light as the very principle and basis of a reformed Christianity. Münzer was saturated with the mystical outlook of the fourteenth century. He read and reread the sermons of John Tauler and he came to the conclusion that there is a Light from God and of God in man's soul which supplies an interior teaching and an anointing from above, and which is the basis of religion, the seat of all spiritual authority. Münzer lacked the necessary balance and solidity to make him an effective reformer in the swirl of events, but he transmitted his *idea* to wiser and saner leaders and this mystical principle found voice and expression in all the books and tracts of the spiritual reformers of that and the next generation. Sebastian Franck (1499-1542), a Swabian chronicler and historian, took up the idea of the inward Light as the true principle of the reformation and did his manly best to give it interpretation, but he had no organising genius and he could not do more than cast his seed forth to germinate later when the soil was prepared for it. He declared that the Word of God, the divine Activity, or the divine Working, the living Power of God, dwells in the soul of man as an inward Light and a Source of guidance.

Franck's influence is profoundly in evidence in Jacob Boehme (1575-1624), one of the great prophets of the inward Light, and it is notable that John Everard (1575-1650), the foremost early English representative of the spiritual reformers, translated Franck's book, *Of the Tree of the Knowledge of Good and Evil*, into English and put it into circulation with other similar mystical translations which he made, together with his own sermons that are full of these mystical ideas. Giles Randall, Francis Rous, William Dell, John Saltmarsh, and Peter Sterry were solid intellectual English interpreters of this interior principle of religion in the period just before Fox began his ministry. Still more important is the fact that all of Jacob Boehme's writings were put into circulation in England in book form between the years 1645 and 1661, and some of his writings had been passed about from hand to hand in script before they were printed. His biography appeared in English as early as 1644 and there was a distinct Boehme cult already under way. It is thus evident enough that George Fox did not originate the principle of the inward Light and it is no less evident that he took up and carried on a teaching that already had received extensive interpretation in books. What was unique and novel in Fox was that he incarnated the idea, became the enthusiastic and effective prophet of it, and with real organising genius made it the living and central principle of a religious Society which he fondly believed was the seed and germ of a new universal Church of Christ in the world.

It must be understood that Fox was not a scholar, as Dr. John Everard was. He had very slender historical perspective. He knew little of his own forerunners. He never tried to think his principle through in any systematic way. He depended on flashes of insight, sudden openings, swift intuitions, and we need not expect to find adequate or consistent interpretations of the principle in his voluminous, but often somewhat confused, books and tracts. Some of his more learned disciples undertook to give it elaborate interpretation, but they were for the most part trained in a Calvinistically

[65]

minded age, and they lacked the mental and spiritual climate in which, by some strange chance or guidance Fox was nurtured.

What we must first see is the fact that Fox, consciously or unconsciously, was making a complete break with Calvinism—that is, with the Reformation as it was formulated in the English Churches of the period. Fox made in 1643 a sharp and momentous revolt from Christianity as he knew it in its existent, established form. He decided to have a different type or none at all. The revolt was almost certainly due to dim, inarticulate ideas which he had already imbibed as a youth from some, now unknown, source. His mind turned strongly away from the theology which he heard from the pulpit and from the hollow religion which failed to transform and empower men's lives. But his new ideas were at first only latent and undeveloped, and it took a long process of clarification before they became for him such explicit and constructive principles as they undoubtedly were by the time he reached Pendle Hill in 1652. He discarded the entire system of Calvinistic theology, because it seemed to him to be a man-made structure, builded up like a new Babel Tower, in the hope that man might climb up to a distant God on this vast structure of intellectual "notions" and "formulations" about Him. These things seemed to Fox to be as hollow and futile for spiritual purposes as pious "works" had seemed to be for Luther, or "the law" had seemed to be for St. Paul. He proposed to make a wholly new start and to make it from the inside rather than from something built up externally. He turned, therefore, to the testimony of *experience*, to God revealed in man's soul.

I cannot find much positive and direct evidence that Fox knew first hand the writings either of the mystics or of the humanists, but his general conception of human nature is an interesting blend of the presuppositions which are taken for granted by these two typical interpretations of man's spiritual nature. Fox accepted, as everybody did, the fact of the "fall" of Adam, and he assumed again, as everybody did, that this "fall" carried with it serious consequences for all the descendants of Adam and for all created nature. He takes for granted, too, as everybody did, that Satan, called by various aliases, is a malignant force working for evil in the universe. But in spite of that common ground of general traditional belief, Fox held a most extraordinarily optimistic view of man and of his possibilities. He himself had shown "gravity and stayedness of mind and spirit" from his early childhood, and he had known "pureness and righteousness" from the time he was eleven years old. He had been overwhelmed with depression at the sin and moral failure which he saw around him, but there is very little sign in the *Journal* of consciousness of sin on his own account. He seems to have felt the grace of God and the fortification of the Spirit in an unusual degree, both keeping him from positive sin and quickly enabling him to recover his peace and reconciliation with God when he did deviate from the true line of march. This rare experience of his own gave him perhaps a somewhat unique confidence in human nature in general. He seems to have believed that every person comes into the world from the creative hand of God with the divine possibility of coming into the condition Adam was in before he fell. The individual himself must no doubt first come up through the flaming sword, through struggle, temptation, and suffering, but the possibility of that victorious attainment lies within the sphere of the will of everyone who is born. Nobody is doomed to go wrong. No one is fated for evil in advance. No person's destiny is rolled off without the consent of his own will. The key to all doors that open into life or into death for man is in his own hands.

Besides this general ground of optimism, Fox came to believe, as his religious views took shape, that a seed of God, an inward Light of divine and heavenly origin, exists within every person who comes into the world, to guide him on all issues of eternal import. "There is something of God in a man," in this man here, in that man there, in the man that is down as well as in the man that is high and lifted up, in the untutored dweller in the forest, and, as well, in the denizen of the city slums, and in the man who is flung into a loathsome dungeon to be forgotten or to be hustled to the gallows, and in the man who is to be sent off in soldier's garb to be a human pawn in the swirl of battle.

A man is not *man*, Fox believed, unless he is free to choose what he will become, unless something in him marks distinctions of good and evil, condemns the wrong course and approves the right one, unless a guiding light, a vision of the ideal path, is possible for him. He certainly cannot be effectively religious unless there is a seed of spiritual life within him that

[69]

can respond to the light and love of God when they break in upon him. His own experience convinced Fox that that spiritual seed of life was the most precious asset of his soul, and it seemed to him that this spiritual seed of life had within itself sublime and immortal capacity of expansion. In fact, he often calls this seed "the Christ within" or "the Spirit of God within us." It has all the potentiality of the Infinite.

It is on this basis that Fox rests his claim that man is the only possible type of *temple* that really has a true holy place or shekinah in it. Buildings, however they are named or "consecrated," remain only material space-occupying structures. They become sacred only through what is done in them by persons who are, by means of the shekinah within them, revealing centres for the life of God. It was on account of his faith in this principle that Fox proclaimed wherever he went that the revelation of God is an unending process. The word of God knows no terminus. The returns are never all in. The book of life is never closed. Man's soul is essentially oracular and prophetic. Fox is usually humble about the quality and range of his own revelations. He does not claim that they are on a level with the revelations given in Scripture. There can be no question of his lofty valuation of the Bible. But he does insist that God speaks to him and through him, and he is confidently certain that God sends him forth to speak prophetic messages to the world. This high conviction of exalted mission was undoubtedly one important factor of his rare personal power over individuals and over groups to whom he spoke.

Furthermore, Fox turned quite naturally to this spiritual principle in man's soul as his new basis of authority in religion. He did not recognize the authority of tradition or of ecclesiastical claims. Nothing could acquire authority merely on account of its age or its prestige. The Church had already ceased in Protestant circles to be regarded as *ipso facto* an ultimate or final authority. Fox took a similar attitude toward the Bible. He refused to call it "the Word of God," for he reserved that exalted phrase to mean the living, eternal, ever-present Christ who alone can, he believed, adequately reveal God. Scripture cannot be used spiritually until it is translated and interpreted, and that work cannot be truly done unless the translator and interpreter possess the same

Spirit that originally gave forth the Scriptures. The Scripture texts do not work by magic, nor as fetishes. They can be used effectively only as they are spiritually apprehended and spiritually applied. That implies and calls once more for the operation of the spiritual seed of life in man. It is just that divine something in the soul which furnishes the true ground of religious authority, precisely as it is an æsthetic quality in the nature of man that enables him to see and appreciate beauty. It means nothing to a dog or cat; it does mean something to a man.

This basis of authority in an individual is not infallible. The Spirit is, of course, thought of as infallible, but any revelation that comes through a finite individual is liable to be warped or coloured by his own peculiar tendencies of thought, traits of character, and unconscious prejudices, though Fox failed to realize to the full the psychological effect of these factors. In the early stage of his public career he was far too apt to consider an urgent suggestion or call or opening to be an infallible divine leading and he did not always distinguish between some great constructive purpose and such an abortive impulse as sent him across the field to cry, "woe

to the bloody city" of Lichfield. And his friend
James Nayler went still farther astray by the
failure to distinguish between impulsive suggestion and wise insight. Fox eventually came to
see that all "openings" and "leadings" need
to be tried and tested by the wider, richer judgment of the spiritual-minded group to which
the individual belongs and in the light of the
lessons of history, and the testimony of the spiritual experience of the race, especially as it is
transmitted to us in Scripture. But even so, the
fact remains that authority to be *authority* must
in the last resort be inwardly felt, apprehended,
appreciated, and accepted.

Fox's whole method of worship was, too, an
outgrowth of his belief in and his experience
of this close intimate inward relation between
God and man. He thought of worship as mutual and reciprocal communion between the human soul and God. The problem is never one
of going somewhere to find a distant or a
hidden God. The problem rather is one of
human preparation for meeting and communing with a God who is always near at hand but
cannot be found and enjoyed until the soul is
ready for such an exalted experience. It means,
therefore, that the worshipper, if he is to enter

into this great attainment, must cease his occu-
pations with external affairs, his thoughts of
house and farm and business, and centre down
into those deeper levels of his being where he
can feel the circulation of spiritual currents and
have healing and refreshment and restoration
and fortification flow in from beyond himself.
This is not worship, but it is preparation for it,
and there comes, with this awareness of the
deeper Life, a palpitating sense of joy and wonder, and a surge of appreciation and adoration
which form the heart of worship. It was in
moments like that in the early apostolic church
that ejaculations of "Abba," "Father," burst
forth from the united congregation, and in the
early Quaker meetings under similar conditions
there came tremulous waves of emotion, which
set the entire group into a state of *quaking*,
from which the name of the movement was
born.[1]

There are, no doubt, other ways of cultivat-
ing and preparing for this sense of presence and
this surge of adoration besides the way which
was most congenial to George Fox and his
friendly groups, but there can be little question
that hush and silence are very effective methods

[1] See above, page 50.

toward that end. It seemed to them that silence in a hushed and expectant group of people worked with more striking effect than did solitary silence for a single lonely worshipper, and this group-silence may be taken as one of the main contributions that George Fox has made to modern religious practice.

It remains only to say in this brief interpretation of the central proclamation of Fox that his faith that there is something of God, a spiritual seed of life, in every man, lay at the very heart of his broad humanitarian spirit. We shall see later that a practical social program sprang out of his faith as naturally as did his method of worship. William Penn said that he was "a divine and a naturalist and all of God Almighty's making." William Penn means by "a divine" a wise expert in spiritual matters. So in fact he was. I am, however, not as confident as William Penn was that he was "a naturalist," an expert in the mysteries of the visible universe. But in any case he had a sure and altogether marvellous way of seeing into human and social problems and of feeling out by a swift intuition the remedy for social ills. His method of approach was the same here as in his method of worship. He felt his way down to a common basis of life, deep-seated in the heart of man.

It was an ancient Hebrew prophet who first had the clear insight that the time would come in happier ages, when God would put his law in man's inward parts and write it in his heart, and a greater than Jeremiah saw that the Kingdom of God could never truly "come" until it was realised as a kingdom formed within men —"the Kingdom of God is within you." George Fox must be reckoned to be one of the religious leaders of the modern world who have most clearly and steadily seen the truth of that principle, and who have been most ready to labour and suffer in order to make it an actual way of life among men.

CHAPTER VI

Margaret Fell of Swarthmore Hall

HARDLY less important than the discovery of the northern Seekers was the meeting of George Fox and Margaret Fell of Swarthmore Hall. Her "convincement" followed close upon their first meeting, and this noble woman became forthwith the nursing mother of the Quaker movement. Her name is almost as intimately bound up with it as is that of Fox himself.

Swarthmore Hall is an Elizabethan manor-house near Ulverston on the edge of the English Lake District. The master of the hall at the time was Thomas Fell, a member of the famous Long Parliament, Judge of Assize of the Chester and North Wales Circuit, Vice-Chancellor of the Duchy and Attorney for the County Palatine of Lancaster. He was about fifty-four years old in 1652, and was one of the most important persons in public life in the north at this period. His wife was sixteen years younger than Judge Fell and ten years older than George Fox. She was a daughter of John Askew of Marsh Grange, and came of a distinguished line of ancestors, though she probably was not a descendant of the martyr, Anne Askew, as has often been claimed. She had married at eighteen and became the mother of nine children, of whom seven daughters and one son, George, were living at the time of Judge Fell's death in 1658.

Margaret Fell had been a seeker in the literal sense of the word for twenty years, though she continued to attend and support the parish church at Ulverston. She had heard rumours of the new movement and had endeavoured to get information of those who were "convinced" in Yorkshire and who were reported to be suffering imprisonment in York. Fox tells us, in his quaint way, that she had had "a vision off a man in a white hatt yt shoulde come and confounde ye preists before my comeinge Into those parts." [1] Fox on his part had already heard that Swarthmore Hall kept "open house" for ministers and for those who had spiritual

[1] *Journal* (Cam. Ed.) i, p. 52.

insight in religious matters, so that he quite naturally turned his feet toward this friendly refuge, as he came from his mountain-top experiences among the Seekers. When he arrived at Swarthmore Hall both Judge Fell and his wife were absent from home, Judge Fell being on the Welsh Circuit and Margaret Fell being temporarily away on some errand. The Ulverston minister at the time was William Lampitt, toward whom Fox always reacted very unfavourably, believing him to be a "Ranter" type of preacher, who made high professions without inward life or truth. "He was full of filth" and "hid his dirty actions" from the family at Swarthmore Hall, is the way the *Journal* presents him to us. Fox had a long personal discussion with Lampitt before he had yet met Margaret Fell, who returned in the evening of the day of his visit to the Hall. He "declared truth" to her and to her family that evening. The next day Lampitt returned for more debate, and Margaret Fell "saw through" her minister as she listened to the discussion with Fox. She was "convinced" of the truth of Fox's message as she heard him search the deep things of life, and with her were "convinced" also all

[79]

of the daughters and most of the family servants.

In all England there were very few women whose "convincement" could have added at that moment more prestige to the cause or more momentum to the movement than did the "convincement" of Margaret Fell. She brought the whole of her life and character to it when she decided to join the new spiritual adventure. She measured the seriousness of the step before she took it and, once she made her decision, it was for life and involved all that she possessed and all that she was or was to be. She was only thirty-eight at the time, though she was already rich in daughters, all of whom she brought into the movement with her. Her husband was a man of great influence in the north and his support and backing, if they were given, were sure to count for much. But the spiritual power and insight and leadership of this dedicated woman was from the first an incalculable asset. There was at the first an emotional element revealed in Margaret Fell's new religious enthusiastic faith that might have proved dangerous. She became almost immediately a *trembleur* and caught the contagion of quaking which was evidently a feature of the early movement in most places.[1] She was carried along into a wave of rapturous religious joy which for a brief period threatened to overcome her usual calm and balance and wisdom, but she very quickly recovered her poise and judgment, and became a remarkable guiding spirit to the ever-widening movement, while Swarthmore Hall soon came to be the central home and headquarters for the large band of "publishers of truth," as the travelling ministers of the new society were called.

Soon after Fox's first arrival at the Hall there was an appointed service at the parish church for "a day of humiliation," and Margaret Fell proposed to attend it, for, as Fox says, "she was not yet wholly come off from them." She asked George Fox to accompany her to the Ulverston service, but he declined to go until he should "feel moved of the Lord" to do so. When Fox finally arrived, Lampitt was in the midst of a hymn. When the hymn was finished, Fox, "moved of the Lord," rose to speak, saying, "He is not a Jew who is one out-

[1] Fox says, significantly, "The Lord's power came upon Margaret Fell and her daughter Sarah and several others." "The Lord's power" appears to me to have been a sudden automatic trembling.—*Journal*, i, p. 121.

wardly, but he is a Jew who is one inwardly."
Then he proceeded to show them that God was
come Himself to teach men within by the Spirit,
calling them away from dead forms and empty
practices and second-hand performances to life
and truth and spirit. Meantime Margaret Fell
had stood up in her pew and was listening, full
of wonder, as she heard him say, "Art thou a
Child of the Light and what thou speakest is it
inwardly from God?" Then she sat down,
weeping, and saying, "We are all thieves; we
have taken the *words* of Scripture, but we know
none of their truths in ourselves." Then she
heard a magistrate order Fox to be removed
from the church, and in the strength of her new
experience she rose in her seat, saying, "Let
him alone. Why may not he speak as well as
any other?" [1] which was her first public align-
ment with "the Children of the Light."

The return of Judge Fell was of course a
crisis. A group of prominent people who were
scandalised by the events of the week hurried
on ahead to meet Judge Fell and to prepare his
mind for what he was to meet on his home-
coming. He was forewarned that Fox had "bewitched" the mistress of Swarthmore Hall, had

[1] *Journal*, i, p. 120; *Ibid*., ii, p. 513.

robbed her of her religion, and had made her a "Quaker." The Judge came to the Hall deeply moved and plainly offended, but he was in control of himself and was man enough not to "break forth into a scene" until he had gathered all the facts before him. Richard Farnsworth and James Nayler were at the Hall when he arrived, though Fox was not there. These two men succeeded in calming Judge Fell's mind so that, as Margaret Fell herself says, "he was pretty moderate and quiet" when he went in for dinner. Margaret sat down by him and was suddenly "seized by the Lord's power" —that is, with trembling, at which the Judge "was stricken with amazement and knew not what to think," but (like the good Judge he was) "was still and quiet." She adds, "The children were all quiet and still and grown sober, and could not play on their music that they were learning, and all these things made him quiet and still." [1]

In the evening, after dinner, Fox arrived, and Judge Fell gave him a full and fair opportunity to present his case. The Judge had heard favourable reports of Fox from Judge Robinson

[1] Margaret Fell's own account is given in the Appendix to the *Journal*, ii, p. 513.

of Yorkshire, and he seemed from the first disposed in his favour. Fox strongly presented his interpretation of Christianity and the Judge listened to it and weighed it carefully. He was apparently dissatisfied with the state of public religion and felt the inward truth and sincerity of Fox. He was not, however, ready to go the whole way to a "convincement," though he became entirely satisfied over the step his wife and family had taken and showed throughout a friendly spirit toward Fox. He gave free permission for meetings to be held in the Hall, and, though he did not attend them in person, he always sat in his study with the door open while the meetings were going on. In fact, as Fox puts it, he was satisfied that the new way was "the way of truth"; he stopped attending church and he used the full force of his influence and his legal skill to protect the new cause.

While Fox was at Swarthmore on a later visit two justices issued a warrant against him, charging him with blasphemy, but, being afraid of Judge Fell, they did not serve the warrant against him. In his usual straightforward manner Fox appeared at the Lancaster sessions to answer the unserved warrant. Judge Fell accompanied him on this occasion, and did much by his legal wisdom and judicial procedure to confound his opponents. It became perfectly evident from this event that Fox had a strong friend in high places and that he could not be overthrown in court by any illicit methods. There were forty "priests" lined up at this trial of Fox, and Judge Fell seemed to be more convinced than ever before that "the truth" was with the new prophet rather than with the old priests.

The "conquest" of Swarthmore Hall was an event of the first magnitude in the life of George Fox—far greater, in fact, than he himself could know at the time. He was, however, at this period close to the edge of ecstasy as he moved from town to town through Lancashire and Westmorland: "So dreadful was the power of God upon me that people flew like chaff before me into their houses. I warned them of the mighty day of the Lord and exhorted them to hearken to the voice of God in their own hearts who was now come to teach His people Himself." [1] At Ulverston, "after the priest was done," he spoke among them the word of the Lord, "which was as a hammer and as a fire amongst them." A graphic picture of his state of

[1] *Journal*, i, p. 125.

mind at the time, taken from the *Short Journal*, shows how near to ecstasy he was and incidentally how much he was like the youthful St. Francis. "I went," he says, "into Kendal market and spoke to the people at the market time. I had silver in my pocket and I was moved to throw it out amongst the people as I was going up the street before I spoke and my life was offered up amongst them." [1]

I shall turn back a little later to deal with Fox's sufferings, inside and outside jails and prisons. For the moment it will be best to follow briefly the remarkable spread of the movement in Bristol and London. This work was not led by Fox in person, but his inspiration animated it and his spirit and method were revealed in it, and it is a part of his story. There was an extraordinary preparation for "the publishers of truth" before they arrived in Bristol. Nowhere else, not even in the northern counties, was there a larger group of dissenting Seekers. Charles Marshall, one of the most remarkable of their number, has left a lucid account of them as follows: "There were many which were seeking after the Lord, and there were a few of us that kept one day of the week in fasting and

[1] The *Short Journal*, p. 21.

prayer; so that when this day came we met together early in the morning, not tasting anything, and sat down sometimes in silence, and as any found a concern on their spirits and inclination in their hearts, they kneeled down and sought the Lord; so that sometimes, before the day ended, there might be twenty of us might pray, men and women, and sometimes children spake a few words in prayer; and we were sometimes greatly bowed and broken before the Lord in humility and tenderness."[1]

John Camm and John Audland, two Westmorland "Seekers," who had been "convinced" by Fox, arrived in Bristol in September, 1654, and an immense pentecostal harvest followed. Their meetings were crowded, sometimes as many as four thousand being present and often as many as three thousand. The entire city was thrown into commotion over the meetings and, as usual, persecution and opposition only added to the list of "convincements." A large number of Quaker leaders came out of the Bristol group, some of whom were strong "publishers." It quickly became one of the largest communities of "the Children of the Light" in England.

Meantime Francis Howgill and Edward

[1] Braithwaite's *Beginnings of Quakerism*, p. 165.

Burrough, two of the most effective of all the band of early preachers, came to London about the same time that Camm and Audland began their harvest in Bristol. Howgill and Burrough must rank among the great fishers of men of the entire group. They pulled in the net with all its meshes strained with the "catch." "By the arm of the Lord," Howgill wrote, "all falls before us, according to the word of the Lord before I came to this city, that all should be as a plain." Burrough is described by an eye-witness standing on a bench in the midst of an immense throng, many in uproar and many contending in opposition, with his Bible in his hand and finishing victoriously with the multitude calm and attentive, convinced by the power of his life as well as by the force of his message. Both these young preachers spoke straight to the hearts and consciences of their hearers. There was life in their words; there was demonstration in their lives. A thousand persons crowded into their "great tavern chapel" as opponents called the "Bull and Mouth Meeting-house," where the early meetings were held, and a very large "convincement" followed.

Fox himself had been in London in the spring of 1655, when he visited Cromwell for the first time, and he had at this time many important interviews with prominent persons and some "great and powerful meetings with throngs of people." Later, after Howgill and Burrough had powerfully "threshed" the city with their preaching, James Nayler came to London and threw himself with zeal and enthusiasm into the work already well under way. The result of all these and many more combined efforts was that the great metropolis, with its multitudinous currents of life, became deeply impregnated with the ideas and practices of the Children of the Light. Swarthmore became the nursing-home, but London soon became the directing centre, of the new movement.

CHAPTER VII

The Sufferings of Fox

"Of Whom the World was Not Worthy"

THE sufferings involved in George Fox's attempt to reconstruct Christianity and to restore it to its primitive life and power were about as great as human nature could bear. It must be said that he took no methods to save himself or to spare himself. He was no doubt often provocative and made himself a shining target for attack. Compromise was not a trait of his character. He never toned down his proclamation to make it more palatable. He never blurred the sharp lines of his dissent from existing ideas and forms. *That* one would not expect of a Puritan-moulded leader. But he went a great deal farther than that. He positively challenged almost every entrenched form and established practice of his time. His break with the Church was complete and he expressed an open hostility to it at almost every point. He thundered against the "priest" of the Church as "an hireling." He set his face as a flint against the entire service of the Church. He swept away all external sacraments. He opposed singing of hymns in public worship. He called the ancient creeds a set of man-made "notions." He so strongly emphasised the divine Light in man's soul that he seemed to his hearers almost to deify man and to discount the exalted position in which the Scriptures were held by all Protestant bodies, though in actual fact he did not under-estimate the value of Scripture. He pushed democratic management to its farthest limit. He gave woman a completely unique status. He carried the doctrine of human equality as far as the "Levellers" did. He said "thou" to every person high or low. He refused to doff his hat to any mortal. Under no circumstances would he take an oath. He utterly refused to have anything to do with war, even war of defence, nor would he sanction the taking of a human life for any reason whatever.

This rigid, unyielding, uncompromising man was bound to be *persona non grata* to multitudes of people wherever he appeared on his travels.

He was furthermore odd-looking, peculiar, and challenging. There was, particularly in the early period, a wave of excitement and a propensity to "horse-play," or to stone-throwing, whenever the rumour spread through a town that "the man in leather breeches had come." Those whose interests were endangered by his teachings quite naturally aroused the mob-spirit in their communities against him, while he himself offered a quite natural provocation to the hoodlum element in any region where his journeys took him. One who breaks as radically as he did with the normal lines and processes of regulated habit might well expect that troubles would rain down upon his head.

These troubles came in two ways. At first they came more especially from the incited mob-spirit and later they came from the action of courts and magistrates in the form of prison sentences. One of his first experiences of man's inhumanity to man came upon him at Mansfield-Woodhouse at the beginning of his mission. "The people fell upon me," he says, "in great rage, struck me down and almost stifled and smothered me; and I was cruelly beaten and bruised by them with their hands and with Bibles and sticks. Then they haled me out, though I was hardly able to stand, and put me into the stocks, where I sat some hours; and they brought dog-whips and horse-whips, threatening to whip me." "Finally," he adds, "the rude people stoned me out of the town for preaching the word of life to them." [1] His journey through Yorkshire in 1652 was marked almost everywhere by brutal assaults. At Tickhill he attempted to speak in the "steeplehouse" (which is his usual word for church), when the clerk struck him in the face with the Bible so that blood gushed from his face. As the crowd got him outside the church they beat him furiously and then threw him over a hedge. Then they dragged him up the street, stoning him and beating him as he was dragged along, covered with blood and with dirt, but as soon as he could get on his feet he "declared the word of life" to them! [2] At Wakefield they rushed upon him, thrust him out of the door, punching and beating him and crying, "Let us have him to the stocks." [3] One of his hardest handlings by a mob occurred in the Island of Walney, off the Lancashire coast, near Furness,

---

[1] *Journal*, i, pp. 45-46. There is a fuller account in *Short Jour.*, p. 12.

[2] *Ibid.*, p. 105.   [3] *Ibid.*, p. 107.

whither he went from Swarthmore at the time
of his first visit in 1652. "Next morning I went
over in a boat to James Lancaster's. As soon as
I came to land, there rushed out about forty
men with staves, clubs, and fishing-poles, who
fell upon me, beating and punching me, and endeavouring to thrust me backward into the sea.
When they had thrust me almost into the sea,
and I saw they would have knocked me down in
it, I went up into the midst of them; but they
laid at me again, and knocked me down, and
stunned me. When I came to myself, I looked
up and saw James Lancaster's wife throwing
stones at my face, and her husband, James Lancaster, was lying over me, to keep the blows and
the stones off me. For the people had persuaded
James Lancaster's wife that I had bewitched
her husband; and had promised her, that if she
would let them know when I came hither, they
would be my death. And having got knowledge
of my coming, many of the town rose up in this
manner with clubs and staves to kill me; but the
Lord's power preserved me, that they could not
take away my life. At length I got up on my
feet, but they beat me down again into the boat;
which James Lancaster observing, he presently
came into it, and set me over the water from

them; but while we were on the water within their reach, they struck at us with long poles and threw stones after us. By the time we were come to the other side, we saw them beating James Nayler; for whilst they had been beating me, he walked up into a field, and they never minded him till I was gone; then they fell upon him, and all their cry was, 'Kill him, kill him.' When I was come over to the town again, on the other side of the water, the townsmen rose up with pitchforks, flails, and staves, to keep me out of the town, crying, 'Kill him, knock him on the head, bring the cart, and carry him away to the churchyard.' So after they had abused me, they drove me some distance out of the town, and there left me." [1]

After a few years of familiarity with the man in leather breeches, and after it became clear to everybody that he was an honest, brave man, working for the rights and privileges of the common people, the mob-spirit died down and Fox and his friends were seldom attacked by street violence. The danger, however, which threatened the movement from the courts and magistrates lasted on until general toleration

[1] *Journal*, i, p. 135.

came with William and Mary in 1689, when
Fox was almost at the end of his life.

I have already noted Fox's first prison experiences. The first taste of prison was in Nottingham in 1649, when he was arrested for
interrupting the sermon and was himself tech-
nically in the wrong. The second incarceration
was in Derby, where he was charged with blasphemy. An act against blasphemy had just been
passed by Parliament in August, 1650. This act
defined blasphemy to be the affirmation by any
mere man that he was God or was equal with
God, or that the Eternal Majesty dwelt in a
mere creature. Fox had used exalted language
about the Christ within him and about perfection, which brought him close to the verge of
danger under the strict interpretation of this
wide blanket act. After the early effusion of his
youth had passed and after he had learned wisdom from the extravagances of others, he was
more cautious and restrained. The second six
months of his year in Derby jail was given to
him on account of his refusal to fight in the
Commonwealth army.

His third imprisonment, which was a very
severe one in Carlisle for seven weeks, came
once more under the charge of blasphemy. They

asked him in court if he was the son of God and he affirmed that he was. He would have claimed that at any time in his life for himself or for any other person who was born anew of the Spirit, but the phrase was loosely open to the interpretation that he was claiming equality with Christ, which he never intended to do. He was thrust into a horrible dungeon among felons and moss-troopers. His surroundings were loathsome. His own account of the conditions are vivid enough to make the picture real: "A filthy nasty place it was, where men and women were put together in a very uncivil manner, and never a house of office to it; and the prisoners were so lousy that one woman was almost eaten to death with lice. Yet bad as the place was, the prisoners were all made very loving and subject to me, and some of them were convinced of the Truth, as the publicans and harlots were of old."[1] His jailers in Carlisle were cruel and his life was plainly put in jeopardy by this commitment. He was charged on this occasion a second time with blasphemy and for a second offence the act carried the penalty of banishment, and failure to leave the Commonwealth involved death by hanging. It

[1] *Journal*, i, p. 171.

was public talk that Fox was to be hanged, for everybody knew that he would never go into banishment unless he was carried away by force. "Great ladies (as they were called)," Fox says, "came to see the man that they said was about to die. While the judge, justices, and sheriff were contriving together how they might put me to death, the Lord disappointed their design by an unexpected way." [1] Justice Anthony Pearson pointed out to the justices of the Carlisle Court that there was no evidence to support the charges against the prisoner, and that he was being illegally held. He was finally dismissed without a formal trial. His release was without doubt hastened by an urgent letter from Parliament (the famous Barebones Parliament) requesting that he be set free.

His fourth imprisonment of eight months in Launceston Castle was the most terrible of all his dungeon experiences, though it was much shorter in time than some of his confinements, and he came out of it in better condition than from the one in Scarborough Castle. His arrest on this occasion was due to the posting of a paper which Fox had written to the seven parishes of Land's End. Major Ceely, the local

[1] *Journal*, i, p. 169.

military representative, came into possession of a copy of the paper, and, under the arbitrary régime of the major-generals, had Fox arrested at St. Ives on the mere suspicion that an un-authenticated traveller who posted public documents might possibly be dangerous. Fox was subjected to scandalous treatment by officers and soldiers as he was being taken to Pendennis Castle. They met General Desborough on the way and a word from him would have instantly released Fox and his two friends, Edward Pyott and William Salt, but he showed no interest, and allowed matters to proceed as they would. The prisoners were then brought to Launceston Castle, January 22, 1656, to wait nine weeks for the court assizes, when they were tried before Chief Justice Glynn. There was a humorous scene in court over the Quaker custom of wearing hats in the presence of the judge, but the judge considered it far from humorous. They were given a heavy fine by the judge for contempt of court, with a sentence of imprisonment until the fine should be paid. Convinced that they were innocent of any crime or violation of law, they refused to pay the fine and were remanded to prison. They were unwilling to pay the jailer his fees for the same reason that they would not pay their fines, whereupon he thrust them into an appalling dungeon called "Doomsdale," which had been used for murderers and witches, and from which few persons had ever come out alive. The horrors of the place are too dreadful for description and the jailer added to the ordinary fierceness of the dungeon by his perverse cruelties. It may well be said that all this appalling experience in "Doomsdale" might have been avoided by a little yielding here or a little finesse there, a little touch of humour, or a little less stiffness of conscience. But Fox was, it must be remembered, the incarnation of a sensitive conscience. No matters of right and wrong could ever be trivial in his sight, and he always assumed, as he stood his lonely ground, that he was fighting and suffering for the rights of the defenceless common man. He was determined, too, never to allow any cost in pain and suffering to keep him from sincerely and honestly living out and practising every truth he taught with his lips.

The sufferings imposed upon the prisoners here in Launceston, as often happens, made the truth of their cause spread. Many from far and near came to see them and to hear their message, and they carried widespread convincements from the very prison in which they seemed likely to be buried. The visitor today at Launceston can see the ruined dungeon where these horrors were endured, and on the wall of the ancient cell of death he reads Fox's brave words, "I was never in prison that it was not the means of bringing multitudes out of their prisons." [1] One man, whose name should be known, Humphrey Norton, went to Oliver Cromwell and offered his body for that of Fox, praying that he might go to Launceston as a substitute for Fox, and if necessary die in his stead. Cromwell, deeply touched by the man's devotion, turned to the members of his Council and asked, "Which of you would do so much for me if I were in the same condition?" Other persons, too, with remarkable loyalty, made similar requests on behalf of Fox. Still the imprisonment dragged on with all its horrors and yet with its touches of heavenly light and love, until the 9th of September, when the prisoners were freed without any payment either of fines or jailer's fees. Out of the vile surroundings and inhuman treatment this unconquerable man

[1] The actual period in "Doomsdale" was not long, perhaps not more than thirteen days, but the entire prison experience was very severe.

[101]

sent the following noble message to his friends: "Let all nations hear the sound by word or writing. Spare no place, spare no tongue nor pen, but be obedient to the Lord God; go through the world and be valiant for the Truth upon earth; tread and trample upon all that is contrary. . . . Be patterns, be examples in all countries, places, islands, nations, wherever you come, that your carriage and life may preach among all sorts of people and to them; *then you will come to walk cheerfully over the world, answering that of God in every one.*"[1]

When Fox walked out of Launceston Castle to go on with his labours, he left behind in these western counties a large number of convinced followers who were to be the centres of many new spiritual communities. Loveday Hambley of Tregangeeves, near St. Austell, was one of the most effective of these awakened spiritual leaders and her home was to become, like Swarthmore Hall in the north, a radiating centre of life. It was now pretty evident that if "Doomsdale" could not frighten, break, or conquer this new challenger, there was no device of man that could turn him from his path of light and truth and duty.

[1] *Journal,* i, pp. 315-317. Italics mine.

The next imprisonment, the fifth, was in Lancaster Castle and was of comparatively short duration, from early June to the end of September, 1660. He was arrested at Swarthmore on a charge of stirring up insurrection against King Charles II, whose "restoration" had just been effected. Fox, after his arrest, was guarded as though he were an extremely dangerous person, some of the soldiers even guarding the fireplace for fear he might magically escape up the chimney! One of the constables declared that he should not have supposed that a thousand men could have taken Fox!

He was charged with being a disturber of the nation and he was denied the privilege of seeing a copy of the *mittimus* on which he was arrested. Judge Fell was no longer living or Fox would have had a noble defender. As it was, he defended himself with much skill and insight. After having made out the prisoner to be a desperately dangerous person, the officials finally allowed him to go up to London unattended by guard or sheriff and without other engagement than his own word of promise that he would appear on a certain day before the London judges. No court could well consider a man very dangerous when he came in unattended and brought in his own hand the charges against himself! Fox finally appealed to the King and his Council for justice, and he was released by an order from Whitehall, dated October 24, 1660, "the Lord's power," as he himself wrote, "having wonderfully wrought for the clearing of my innocency." [1]

I shall pass over his short imprisonment of one month at Leicester, beginning early in September, 1662, for refusing to take the Oath of Supremacy and Allegiance, and come at once to the seventh one—the longest of his life— beginning at Lancaster early in 1664 and finishing at Scarborough, September, 1666, a period of two years and eight months. A definite act against the Quakers was passed by Parliament and received the King's signature in May, 1662. It was aimed against their opposition to oaths, their meeting in great numbers, and their maintenance of extensive correspondence with one another. This act at once brought a storm of persecution upon Friends in all parts of the Kingdom. The Fifth Monarchy rising in January, 1661, had had the general effect of arousing widespread suspicion of plots and uprisings, and Friends had a heavy harvest of

[1] *Journal*, i, pp. 473-488.

trouble from an event in which they had no part and with which they felt no manner of sympathy.

Meantime a magistrate named Daniel Fleming, of Rydal Hall, Westmorland, offered a reward of five pounds for the capture of George Fox, and at Fleming's instigation Fox was arrested in January, 1664, soon after his arrival at Swarthmore Hall. He was brought to Holker Hall, the home of Justice Preston, where he had a preliminary hearing and gave his promise to appear before the Lancaster Quarter Sessions. Fox was present at the Sessions on January 12, and once more had trouble over his failure to remove his hat. He was tendered the Oath of Supremacy and Allegiance, and of course refused it. He was then committed to prison, and so, too, were Margaret Fell and many other Friends.

Fox's trial dragged on through assize after assize in the Lancaster courts. He found grave errors in the indictment against him and would have had release had not the judge at each crisis asked him to take the oath, which each time he refused, and thus for fourteen months he was kept in Lancaster Castle and treated as a praemunired person, though he was never so

sentenced in open court. Margaret Fell meantime did receive an actual sentence of outlawry,
under the law of praemunire, which put her out
of the King's protection and condemned her to
life-long imprisonment, with loss of all her
property. Through the King's intervention she
served only four and a half years of imprisonment and eventually recovered her estate.
Both Fox and Margaret Fell rose to their full
height of moral grandeur during these harrowing months. On one occasion during the trial
Fox had a striking ecstatic experience with a
sense of divine presence.

When final sentence was rendered in Fox's
case he was condemned to be removed from
Lancaster and to be carried across country to
Scarborough for an indeterminate period of confinement. Weak and hardly able to stand alone
from his sufferings in the Lancaster prison, Fox
was carried on horseback in June, 1665, to Scarborough Castle, where for sixteen months he
was "as a man buried alive." He was put into
an open room in the Castle "where the rain
came in and which was exceedingly thick with
smoke." "One day," he says, "the Governor,
Sir Jordan Crosland, came to see me and
brought with him Sir Francis Cobb. I desired

the Governor to go into my room and see what a place I had. I had got a little fire made in it, and it was so filled with smoke that when they were in they could hardly find their way out again; and he being a Papist, I told him that this was his Purgatory which they had put me into."

He was soon moved to much worse quarters where there was neither chimney nor fire-hearth. It being toward the seaside, opening out on the North Sea and without protection over the opening, "the wind drove in the rain forcibly," he says, "so that the water came over my bed and ran so about the room that I was fain to skim it up with a platter. When my clothes were wet, I had no fire to dry them; so that my body was benumbed with cold, and my fingers swelled so that one was grown as big as two." Fox never altogether recovered his full health after these terrible exposures from the North Sea storms, which beat into his cell and kept his clothes drenched for long periods at a time.[1]

Few of his friends were allowed to see him, but many curious sightseers came to gaze on him in his misery, and many opponents of his

[1] *Journal,* ii, pp. 58-70.

views came to debate with him. In the heat of debate he found warmth and entertainment and he was ready and keen for any theological assaults and could forget his woes in argument. Gradually Sir Jordan Crosland took his spiritual measure and became interested in him and friendly toward him. After he had lain in Scarborough for over a year he sent a letter to King Charles, giving him an account of his imprisonment and his sufferings. Friends of his also used their good offices at Court and finally an order of release was procured from the King and Fox was set free without giving bond or surety. The governor of the castle gave him a letter of discharge and treated him with respect and affection, while the officers and soldiers in the castle gave this comment on their late prisoner: "He was as stiff as a tree, and as pure as a bell, for we could never bow him" [*i. e.*, bend him]. Fox went some years later to visit his former keeper and was "received very courteously and lovingly." The discharge came September 1, 1666, the day before the outbreak of the Great London Fire.

His last imprisonment, the eighth, was begun in Worcester, December 17, 1673, and ended in London fourteen months later, February 12,

1675. He had landed at Bristol from his American journey in June, 1673; he had visited Friends in that region, he had made a tour of the London meetings and was on his way to visit his elderly mother, now seriously ill at Fenny Drayton, when he was arrested at Armscott and taken to the county jail in Worcester, with Thomas Lower, son-in-law of Margaret Fell, for companion. They were brought before the Quarter Sessions, January 21, 1674.[1] The justices seemed plainly embarrassed as the prisoner came in and they "were stricken with paleness in their faces." There was in reality no case against the prisoners, but at the suggestion of a "priest" they were asked to take the customary oath, by which, of course, they were "caught," and were remanded to prison. Under a *habeas corpus* proceeding Fox went up to London and spent some weeks. He attended Yearly Meeting in June, 1674, but at the next sessions he was given a sentence of praemunire and put back into Worcester jail. After six months he was taken to London on another *habeas corpus*, and tried before the famous Lord Chief Justice,

[1] The account in this chapter, of Fox's experiences with courts, does not give all the appearances at Quarter Sessions nor all the releases.

[109]

Sir Matthew Hale, who quashed the indictment and refused this time to put the oath to him, giving as his reason that he had "heard many good reports" of Fox. This ended his last prison experience. His mother had died while he was confined in the jail, and his words of love and grief over her passing were most tender and touching.

His own health broke once more while he was going through this last imprisonment, and many Friends doubted of his recovery, but "lying awake one night," he says, "upon my bed in the glory of the Lord, which was over all, it was said unto me that the Lord had a great deal more work for me to do for Him before He took me to Himself."

One of the fortunate features of these long prison interruptions to Fox's labors and travels was the quiet opportunity they offered for the composition of the story of his life and his work. It seems improbable that we should ever have got any continuous biographical story if it had not been for the periods of forced confinement. His so-called *Short Journal*, the earliest personal narrative of his life, was written while he was in Lancaster jail in 1663-64, before he was taken across country to Scarborough. The original manuscript with its vivid pictures of his early experiences and sufferings was probably dictated to some amanuensis during this long hard period in prison, though it may have been first written by his own hand and later copied at Swarthmore Hall in "the little oblong volume" now to be seen in the Library at Friends House, London. It was edited and printed as a memorial volume on the occasion of the tercentenary of his birth.

The *Great Journal*, which formed the main document from which Thomas Ellwood produced the well-known *Journal of George Fox* after his death, was begun and largely composed in Worcester jail. The work was almost entirely dictated by Fox and written down by Thomas Lower, his prison companion. It was later carried on and completed up to the year 1675 at Swarthmore Hall. The rest of the *Journal* material consisted of "Travel Diaries" written from time to time by companions of travel or attendant secretaries.[1] Thomas Ellwood omitted many passages from the original

[1] Some of these "Travel Diaries" are included in the Tercentenary Volume. The original of the *Great Journal* was edited by Norman Penney, F.S.A., and published by the Cambridge Press in 1911.

Great Journal, and toned down others to a so-berer hue, casting the whole work in a slightly more refined literary form. The *Journal of George Fox* as it came from Thomas Ellwood's hand is a unique autobiography. It is too bulky for the general reader and it contains passages and sections which now seem dry and wooden, particularly the pages that deal with the years after 1675. But the vital parts of the *Journal* are still fresh with the throbbing life of a rugged, honest, original, and prophetic man, who did his life-work in noble fashion and who showed heroic fibre throughout his difficult career. It contains, in vigorous elevated style, the precious story of a great spiritual reformer and social liberator.

Severe as were the sufferings of Fox in these eight imprisonments which I have only briefly reviewed, many of his followers and friends had still severer experiences to go through and large numbers of them laid down their lives in prison in obedience to their faith. It seems rather strange that he, being as he was the out-standing figure in the movement, should have come through the perils, dangers, and suffer-ings alive and should have survived the long period of intense persecution. It is a notable fact that it is reckoned that he was arrested or haled before courts or magistrates no less than sixty times during his lifetime. The eight imprisonments are, therefore, only a small part of what might have been inflicted upon him since his refusal to take an oath or to remove his hat was always ground enough for a conviction without terminal limits.

CHAPTER VIII

Fox and Cromwell

IT WOULD be difficult to find in any one generation in any one country two more unique and original characters than George Fox and Oliver Cromwell. They were very unlike in most aspects of their natures and their missions. But they were both intensely religious men. They were both conscious of being divinely chosen to do a great work for the Almighty. They both felt a tremendous sense of awe in their attitude and relation to Him. In a loose use of the word, they were both *mystics*. Cromwell had grown up under stern Puritan views of life and conceptions of God, but there were great moments in his later life when he knew the reality of God as a fact of experience and not merely because he read about Him in books or heard ordained divines preach about Him. He moved gradually away from the religious position of his early life toward a freer and less rigid basis. In fact, there was a strong Seeker strain in his later life and a pronounced tendency toward independency and a genuine sympathy with it. Lord Rosebery is undoubtedly right when he calls Cromwell a "practical mystic," by which he means a person who carried a Sinai in his own soul and who with awe and reverence practised the presence of God, though without being quite clearly *conscious* of that presence, in the sense that the great mystics of history have been.

Fox and Cromwell ought to have understood and appreciated one another, and up to a certain point they did each understand and appreciate the other, but the exigencies and demands of Cromwell's difficult rôle and position made him suspicious of all contagious popular movements, and he more or less mistrusted the Quaker doctrine of the inner Light because it seemed to him to be too closely allied with the wild claims of the contemporary Ranters. There were, however, some striking and impressive contacts between the two men.

Their first meeting together occurred in March, 1655. The Protector, who had at this time held his office for about six months, had been informed in February that the Cavaliers and Quakers were joining together in a plot to rise in arms against him. It was absurd enough, but almost anything can be believed in times of fear and propaganda. Accordingly, Fox was arrested at Whetstone by Colonel Hacker and taken, as we have seen in an earlier chapter, to Leicester. Colonel Hacker soon saw that there was no real danger to be feared from this religious leader, and he was ready to let him go free if he would give a promise not to hold meetings, since popular meetings did present a real danger. Of course Fox refused to give such a promise and was consequently sent up to London in charge of Captain Drury. Here he issued a remarkable declaration in which he said: "I, who am of the world called George Fox, do deny the carrying or drawing of any carnal sword against any, or against thee, Oliver Cromwell, or any man. In the presence of the Lord God I declare it, God is my witness."

Fox's document was taken to the Protector, who read it and directed Captain Drury to bring his prisoner to Whitehall for an interview. It was a memorable scene and would make a notable picture if any artist could reproduce it. Fox arrived in the early morning before Cromwell was dressed. The Quaker leader was ushered into the presence of the great soldier and ruler and was "moved" to say, "Peace be in this house"—a house that had not been noted in the past as an habitation of peace! He then exhorted the Protector to "keep in the fear of the Lord that by it he might be directed and order all things under his hand to God's glory." "I spoke to him of Truth," says the new prophet, in his modest account of the visit, "and I had much discourse with him about religion." "He carried himself very moderately," Fox reports, "but he said that we quarrelled with priests, whom he called ministers." Quite naturally Fox insisted that the "priests" began the quarrel and that Friends would be gentle toward them if they would give evidence that they were apostolic and Christ-sent men. Then Fox launched out into an attack on the "hireling" aspect of the established clergy and contrasted that trait in their lives with the spirit of the great prophets and apostles who gave their messages "freely" at great cost to themselves. Several times Cromwell ejaculated, "That is true! That is very good!"

"Many more words I had with him, but people coming in, I drew back a little," the *Journal* goes on to say. "As I was turning, he caught me by the hand and with tears in his eyes said, 'Come again to my house; for if thou and I were but an hour of a day together we should be nearer one to the other'—and he added, 'I wish no more ill to thee than I do to my own soul.' "[1] Carlyle, commenting on this extraordinary scene, says, "Yes, George, this Protector has a sympathy with the Perennial; and feels it across the Temporary: no hulls, leathern or other, can entirely hide it from the sense of him."[2]

Before he actually left the Protector's room, Fox stepped closer to the great man and admonished him to "hearken to God's voice that he might stand in His counsel and obey it." "If thou dost hearken to that voice," he solemnly declared, "it will keep thee from hardness of heart and if thou dost not hear God's voice thy heart will be hardened." "That is true," Cromwell answered, as one who quite obviously felt that he was listening to the words of a real prophet. There can be no question that the advice was sound and appropriate. Fox had come in as a prisoner in charge of a guard, but he had

[1] *Journal,* i, p. 210.
[2] *Oliver Cromwell, Letters and Speeches* (Cent. Ed.) vol. iii, p. 225.

conducted himself throughout as a person bearing a message from the Lord and when he had finished the Protector told him that he was at full liberty to go where he would as a free man. He was taken to the Great Hall, where the Protector's gentlemen were entertained, and he was told that Cromwell wished him to dine in the Hall with his gentlemen. "Tell the Protector," Fox replied, "that I did not come here to eat his food or to drink his drink." When Cromwell heard this report of Fox's independent attitude and his refusal to accept the entertainment, he said to some of his attendants, "Now I see that there is a people risen and come up that I cannot win with gifts or honours, offices, or places; but all other sects and people I can." [1]

Thus ended the first meeting of these two remarkable Englishmen. It is plain enough that they had at this time a genuine mutual respect and a certain quiet admiration. It continued for some months, but one can see that Fox gradually grows less appreciative as Cromwell becomes more absolute in authority and he takes on a somewhat sterner attitude toward the man who held the destiny of so many persons and so many issues in his hand. He blames him espe-

[1] *Journal,* i, pp. 210-211.

cially for not being more concerned to safeguard liberty of conscience, and to give wider scope to freedom for religious thought. He comes eventually to the conclusion that Cromwell was largely responsible for the sufferings of the "saints in prison" and for the persecuting spirit of the times. He is peculiarly opposed to Cromwell's frequent proclamations for national fasts. On one of these occasions, when a fast was proclaimed to pray for rain, Fox wrote to the Protector that he would have plenty of rain throughout the nation if he would "own God's Truth," that the drought was only a visible sign of inward barrenness and lack of the water of life. He pointed out further in his letter that there was plenty of rain in the regions where "truth had spread"—that is to say, where the Children of the Light dwelt!

The second interview with Cromwell was in 1656 and was unexpected and unpremeditated. Fox was returning to London from great meetings in Bristol, and when he came to Hyde Park he saw "a great clutter of people" and then espied Oliver Cromwell coming in his coach. "Whereupon," Fox says, "I rode to his coachside. Some of his life-guard would have put me away; but he forbade them. So I rode by his coach-side with him, declaring what the Lord gave me to say to him, of his condition, and of the sufferings of Friends in the nation, showing him how contrary this persecution was to the words of Christ and His apostles and to Christianity. When we were come to James's Park Gate, I left him; and at parting he desired me to come to his house." [1] Cromwell, on his return to the palace, told Mary Saunders, one of his wife's maids, who was a Quaker, that he had good news to bring her, "George Fox has come to town," and then the Protector described to the maid how Fox had met him and had ridden through the park alongside his coach.

A little later Fox and his friend, Edward Pyott, went to Whitehall to see Cromwell, in accordance with the parting invitation in Hyde Park. Fox referred once more to the sufferings of Friends throughout the nation, and urged him to live in and obey the Light of Christ. Cromwell said that this was a natural light, but Fox proceeded to interpret it in his usual fashion as being divine and heavenly, coming from the new and spiritual man, Christ Jesus, the Light and Life of God. Then Fox felt the power of God arise in him in a special manner

[1] *Journal*, i, p. 332.

and he was "moved" to bid the Protector "lay down his crown at the feet of Jesus." Fox evidently on this occasion rose to the full height of what he believed to be his prophetic function and poured out a message which seemed given him from God, but it did not meet the response in Cromwell's soul that Fox expected. The Protector "spoke in a light manner" and went on opposing the doctrine of the inner Light, though afterwards, when Fox had departed, Cromwell felt compunctions for his treatment of his visitor and is reported to have said to his wife, "I never parted from George Fox that way before." [1] The failure of the visit and the neglect of his message plainly left a deep impression on Fox's mind, and from this time forward his tone is somewhat altered toward the Protector. He says significantly toward the end of 1656: "At this time O. P. (Oliver Protector) begann to harden, and severall freinds were turned out of there offices." [2]

At the crisis of his Protectorate, when many were urging Cromwell to take the title of king and when he himself seemed inclined to accept the crown, Fox "felt moved" to go to him and warn him against accepting it. "I mett him in

[1] *Journal,* i, p. 333. [2] *Cambridge Journal,* i, p. 263.

ye parke," the quaint account says, "and tolde him yt they yt would putt him on a crowne woulde take away his life: and hee askt mee what did I say: and I said againe they yt sought to putt him on a crowne woulde take away his life: and I bidd him minde ye crowne yt was immortal and hee thankt mee and bid mee goe to his house." [1] Fox wrote several letters to Cromwell about the crown and about Friends' sufferings and about futile "fasts," but the old intimate tone had passed. One of his letters dealt with the famous fast of humiliation in connection with the Protestant sufferings in the Piedmont Valleys—a persecution which called forth Milton's great sonnet,

Avenge, O Lord, thy slaughtered saints whose bones
Lie scattered on the Alpine mountains cold.

Fox endeavoured to explain to Cromwell the true nature of a "fast" and reminded the Protector that instead of blaming Papists for persecuting Protestants on the Continent, he would do well to search his own soul and ask himself whether *he* was doing right in persecuting "friends and neighbours at home."

[1] *Ibid.*, i, p. 267.

One of Fox's most intimate and tender letters was sent sometime in 1658 to Lady Claypole, Cromwell's second daughter, Elizabeth. She was married in 1646 to John (afterwards Lord) Claypole, whose brother James was a Friend. Elizabeth Cromwell had for many years been dissatisfied with the Christianity which she heard preached and saw practised in the world of her time. The year of her marriage Cromwell had written about her in these remarkable words: "Shee is exercised with some perplexed thoughts and sees her own vanitye and carnal mind; bewailing it, shee seekes after that wch will satisfie, and thus to be a Seeker is to be of the best sect next to a Finder, and such shall every faithful, humble Seeker be at the end." She evidently did not become a happy Finder until the very end of her life. Fox says of her in 1658, twelve years after her father's letter, "She was much troubled in mind and could receive no comfort from any that came to her." It was under these circumstances during her final illness that Fox felt moved to write to her.

"Keep in the fear of the Lord God," he wrote. "All these things happen to thee for thy good and for the good of those concerned for thee, to make you know yourselves and your

[124]

weakness, that ye may know the Lord's strength and power and may trust in Him. Keep low in His fear that thereby ye may receive the secrets of God and His wisdom and may know the shadow of the Almighty and sit under it in all tempests, storms and heats. For God is *a God at hand*. Look at the Light which discovers your sins and you will see over them. That will give victory and ye will find grace and strength; that is the first step to peace. Come to know the seed of God, which is the heir of the promise of God and of the world that hath no end, that ye may feel the power of an endless life, the power of God which is immortal, which brings the immortal soul up to the immortal God, in whom it doth rejoice. So in the name and power of the Lord Jesus Christ, God Almighty strengthen thee. G. F." [1]

There is one more contact to report between Fox and Cromwell and one strange scene after the death of the Protector. A short time before Cromwell's death Fox saw him and had his last interview with him. His own description of it

[1] Somewhat abbreviated from the original letter written in seventeenth-century phraseology, but there are tenderness and spiritual insight in the simple message and we need not be surprised to learn that it "stayed her mind."

deserves to be quoted: "Taking boat, I went to Kingston and thence to Hampton Court, to speak with the Protector about the sufferings of Friends. I met him riding in Hampton Court Park and before I came to him, as he rode at the head of his life-guard, I saw and felt a waft of death go forth against him; and when I came to him he looked like a dead man." [1] Fox was peculiarly sensitive to the states of mind of those whom he met and he was on many occasions pretty clearly in telepathic *rapport* with the mental condition of his friends and others who were passing through sufferings. This unusual word "waft" is probably used, as Defoe and other seventeenth-century writers use it, to mean *a signal*, given to the beholders perhaps in the form of an apparition of death, or it may be only as the waft of a current or breath of air. Cromwell's death occurred on September 3, 1658, but, unfortunately, we cannot accurately date the "waft," though it would appear to have been perceived a very short time before the end came to Cromwell.

Fox goes on to say in his account, "After I had laid the sufferings of Friends before him and had warned him, according as I was moved

[1] *Journal*, i, p. 440.

to speak to him, he bade me come to his house. So I returned to Kingston, and the next day went to Hampton Court, to speak further with him. But when I came he was sick, and Harvey, who was one that waited on him, told me the doctors were not willing I should speak with him. So I passed away and never saw him more." [1]

In his manuscript *Journal* (now printed as the *Cambridge Journal*) Fox recorded an incident which Thomas Ellwood quite naturally omitted when he edited the *Journal* in its final form. He said, "O. C. at Dunbar fight promised to ye Lord yt if hee gave him ye victory, over his enmys hee woulde take away tythes, etc. or else lett him bee rowled Into his grave with Infamy. But when ye Lord had given him ye victory and hee came to be cheife hee confirmed ye former lawes yt if people did not sett forth there tythes, they shoulde pay treble." Then follow the words which record the final scene: "Butt when ye Kinge came in they tooke him (Cromwell) uppe and hanged him: and buryed him under Tyburn where he was rowled Into his grave with Infamy. And when I saw him hanginge there I saw his worde Justly come upon him." [1]

One regrets that the tone is not gentler here and that the dreadful scene which occurred at the Restoration did not move Fox with solemn respect and reverence rather than with a stern sense of judgment. But it is difficult even for great prophet souls to rise above natural human feelings and to see with eyes of love as saints and angels see. Fox was always too much concerned with "judgments," and he had too keen an eye for the retributions which fell upon those who persecuted the Lord's people.

He had come to feel toward the end of the Protectorate that Cromwell was responsible for the sufferings of Friends and his own heart hardened toward the man who seemed to him to be growing hard. Anthony Pearson, one of Fox's finest disciples, declared after an interview with Cromwell: "There was not ye least signe of any honesty left in him nor any tendernesse though I spoke enough to have broken his heart." [2] That was the way Friends generally felt toward the man from whom they had hoped so much.

[1] *Cambridge Journal*, i, p. 385.
[2] See *Cambridge Journal*, i, p. 456.

Cromwell, we may conclude, was impressed by the rugged honesty and sincerity of Fox. He seems to have felt that there was a genuine strain of the prophet in the odd Quaker leader who came so often to warn him and to counsel him at crises in his life. But he held a delicate position in which finesse and balance and compromise seemed necessary. Fear of plots and risings was always present in the back of his mind. The air was full of heresies and schisms that offended the sterner puritanic element in the nation, and lenient toleration of inner Light prophets would have wrecked the Protectorate in its infancy. But there was nothing of the politician in the Fenny Drayton prophet and he could see only hardness of heart in the man who refused to abolish tithes, who tolerated "priests," and who allowed Quakers to languish and die in filthy prisons.

CHAPTER IX

Organising the Movement

IN NOTHING did George Fox show the mark of genius more distinctly than in the way he worked out the organisation of his movement and adjusted it to fit his religious ideals. He quite obviously shared in his early period the position of the spiritual reformers. They discounted the value of organisation and were decidedly afraid of it. They were impressed with the fact that organisation only too easily becomes an end in itself and threatens to mask, if it does not supplant, the primary spiritual aims of the movement itself. Then it is sure to produce and foster a group of persons who become its managers and manipulators, who live on it, tend to house themselves in it like parasites, and grow to be the conservative guardians of its forms and customs and manners. In their fear of the deadening effects of ecclesiasticism and the *arresting* tendency of any type of organisation, these spiritual reformers risked the spread of their precious seed of truth, as Christ seems to have done, on the principle of personal contagion. They believed that one life saturated with light and love would transmit those spiritual forces and produce a hundred more centres of radiance and grace. Instead, then, of an organisation they would have an organism. Instead of machinery they would have life. Instead of a visible church they would have an invisible one.

Fox, I say, seems at first to have shared this view. In the beginning of his mission he announced the principle that "if one man or woman were raised by God's power to stand and live in the same Spirit that the prophets and apostles were in who gave forth the Scriptures, that man or woman should shake all the country in their profession for ten miles round." [1] That amounts to the statement that a hundred-horse-power person will raise the spiritual level of a multitude of other persons who before were merely nominal in their profession and lacking a dynamic quality. In the period when the little band bore the name "Children of Light" there was no sign of eagerness for organisation or per-

[1] *Journal*, i, p. 109.

manent construction. Contagion there was and transmission of life, but no thought for the morrow, or of the building of barns to hold the grain that was harvested.

As the work spread, however, out into wider fields and as the large numbers of the Seekers came in to swell the movement, there had to be some thought of future planning and some kind of system. Persecution and suffering compelled the leaders of the movement to take some measures of relief for those who were in prison and for families that were deprived of the breadwinner and the care-taker. Then there were disorders to be straightened out and disturbers to be restrained or at least to be dealt with. The disaster of James Nayler's aberration and excessive claims of divinity suddenly and startlingly revealed the dangers that lay concealed in a movement which glorified subjectivism and inner impulses and which failed to provide a real basis of authority.[1]

They were, furthermore, confronted with the urgent problem of finding some proper way to

[1] Fox's brief account of Nayler's aberration is given in the *Journal*, i, p. 327. The account of his own apparently misguided mission to the city of Lichfield is given in the *Journal*, i, p. 77.

solemnise marriages. Quite obviously those who joined the new movement saw from the first that they could not accept the services of a "priest" on occasions of marriage, nor could they be satisfied with a civil marriage. The joining of two lives in marriage seemed to them to be an event of the holiest and most sacred order and therefore it must be accomplished in spirit and in truth as an act of worship or as a sacrament of life. Here were matters that called for a statesman as well as a prophet and mystic, and Fox proved equal to the occasion.

There were two stages in the process of developing the organisation. The first stage was marked by an uttermost degree of simplicity; the second stage was somewhat more developed and explicit. The first stage was in the main one of personal leadership and inspiration; the second was far more organic and group-centered. The first stage covers the years from 1656 to 1660; the second stage began with Fox's release from Scarborough Castle in 1666 and runs on to the end of his life. Already before 1656 there had been the germs of an organisation. Those who were "convinced" met together to wait upon the Lord, to worship, to praise, and to edify one another. Dominating personalities, as happens everywhere, came to the front and exercised their influence. The local leaders consulted together and worked out simple arrangements for the matters in hand. As soon as Fox was released from Launceston in September, 1656, he proceeded during the next few months to hold three important General Meetings in the southern counties for purposes of inspiration, fellowship, and incipient organisation. A more important General Meeting was held at Balby in Yorkshire in November, proposed and inspired by Fox, but not attended by him. Leaders from all sections of Yorkshire and from Derby, Lincoln, and Nottingham were present and took forward, practical steps in the direction of methods and discipline. Similar meetings were held in other parts of England, and a tiny, more or less fluid, working plan emerged. Sometime in the summer of 1657 Fox apparently called a conference of leaders from the counties to meet with him at Swarthmore to set up meetings for the conduct of the affairs of the spiritual groups and to arrange for a General Meeting at Skipton in Yorkshire a little later that same year. These Skipton meetings continued annually until 1660 and were the real nursery of the incipient organisation which soon came to be known as the Society of Friends.[1] The meeting for 1658, which was held at Scalehouse, near Skipton, was a very important stage in the organising process, and it was marked by an inspiring outlook over the lands to be conquered. Ten counties were represented at this meeting.

By these methods plans were worked out for holding meetings for worship and for the simple affairs of business. Steps were taken for recording births and deaths. Provision was made for collections to care for the poor, for those in prison and for those who were engaged in "publishing truth." Arrangements were drawn up for dealing with "those who walked disorderly" and for the general care of the flock, and the admirably simple form of Quaker marriage took shape.

Fox's model type of marriage was that of Adam and Eve before the Fall. In this noble instance there was no "priest" and no magistrate present; unfortunately for Fox's system, there were no witnesses, either! He assumed, however, that Adam stood up and took his new-formed bride by the hand and "in the presence

[1] See *Cambridge Journal*, i, p. 266. W. C. Braithwaite's excellent chapter on Organization should be read in *Beginnings of Quakerism*.

of the Lord" they plighted their love and faith to one another and thus married themselves. It was Adam's "forme of wordes," somewhat imaginatively reproduced, that Fox adopted for the marriages of Friends. "In the presence of the Lord and these our Friends I take thee to be my wife, promising by divine assistance to be unto thee a loving and faithful husband," were the simple words of affectionate promise, and the maiden responded in like manner. The witnesses signed a certificate which the bridegroom and bride had previously signed in public meeting. And to avoid irregularities the parties intending marriage were to signify their proposal to the meeting in advance, to satisfy Friends that they were clear of other attachments and had the proper consent of parents, and then a committee of Friends was appointed to attend the meeting in which the marriage was to occur, and to form part of the group of witnesses. Fox gave out a paper of advice on marriage as early as 1653, and in later advices, recorded in his *Journal*, asked Friends to "lay their intentions before the faithful before anything was concluded and afterwards publish it in the end of a meeting, or in a market, as they were moved thereto."

The validity of this simple form of marriage was legally established by a decision of court in 1661 in a Nottingham case. The judge on this occasion explained to the jury, almost in the words of Fox, how there was a marriage in Paradise when Adam took Eve and Eve took Adam, and, he concluded, "it is the consent of the parties that makes a marriage." So in fact the court decided. This Nottingham decision, however, was not the end of the matter, but the principle here enunciated has finally prevailed and now has legal status in most Anglo-Saxon countries. The only advance that has been made over the practice of Adam and Eve in Paradise is that there must be witnesses and the act must be recorded. One characteristic piece of advice comes from Fox which insists in his straightforward way on frank sincerity: "No man or woman [is] to speak anything but that they do uprightly and faithfully intend to perform in all things."

Even the simple early stage of organisation, loose and inchoate as it was, aroused opposition and produced a spirit of resistance. Some who had joined the new movement looked upon any form or method or rules as a yoke of bondage. They wanted absolute liberty and they regarded any outside authority as an interference with the free flow of the Spirit. John Perrot was the incarnation of this type of unrestricted freedom. He had gone out in 1657 with holy fervour to convert the Orient to the truth of the Light within, and on his way back from the Near East he fell into the hands of the Inquisition in Rome and was committed to a mad-house for three years. The only thing that saved his life was the merciful decision that he was mentally disordered, which was probably not far from the truth. On his return to England from Rome in 1660 Perrot pushed his abstract and negative mysticism to an extreme limit, declaring that it is now "the purpose of God to bring to naught all the customary, traditional ways of worship of the sons of men." He struck first at the Quaker custom of removing hats when prayer was vocally offered, and he went on to oppose all human arrangements for public meetings, claiming that everything should be left to direct "movings and openings" made to the individual soul on the occasion, including the time and place at which meetings should be held. Perrot might have been considered negligible had it not been for the fact that his self-sacrificing labours and his suffer-

ings for the cause of truth and his holy life
had given him prestige, and had he not carried
some prominent persons over into sympathy
with his extreme mysticism and his abstract liberty. This and other unsettling influences and
episodes had by 1666 produced an ominous situation which called for wise and careful handling. When Fox came back to life and action
after having been buried for three years in
Lancaster Prison and Scarborough Castle he
found one of the major tasks of his life waiting
for him. Fortunately, his practical sense and
sound judgment were all well developed, as
was his mystical insight, and he now showed
that he could construct, as well as enjoy visions.
He was now a man forty-two years old, at the
moment prematurely broken in health, but
capable of recovery and of immense endurance
and labour. He had been consulting, reflecting,
meditating and drawing upon higher wisdom
during his long silent months in prison, and he
came forth with his plans formed for reviving
and fortifying his widespread fellowship and
making the body more effective and efficient by
increased consolidation and wider group control.

His instrument for the new creative work
was the Monthly Meeting. It was a district con-

gregational meeting for the oversight and guidance of the members of near-by local meetings. At first the Monthly Meeting was composed entirely of men, but Fox, with his noble theory of equality of the sexes in all spiritual matters, soon added Women's Meetings to his original scheme. The congregational range and scope of the Monthly Meeting were not at its birth quite equal to those of the early Brownist meetings, but it contained the vital seeds of a real democracy, and out of the simple experiment came eventually a very rich and fertile type of group control and direction, which developed a procedure without voting and without majority and minority sectors. In some places the district meeting was held four times a year instead of once each month, but when the pattern of organisation was brought to completion the Quarterly Meeting became a superior meeting over the Monthly Meeting, involving the affairs of all the Monthly Meetings of a county, while over these larger district meetings was the sphere of the General Meetings for the whole country, which soon came to be called the Yearly Meeting.

Up and down the country, on foot or on horseback, Fox travelled, rallying the members together, giving them messages of edification, and then explaining to them the scope and function of the Monthly Meeting and staying in each region until the plan was launched in an experimental meeting with its inevitable record book of the proceedings. One of the early record books says: "At this meeting was our dear friend and elder brother in the Truth, George Fox, who was then travelling through the nation, being moved of the Lord thereunto, in order to the settling of both Monthly and Quarterly Meetings in their respective counties, which work the Lord blessed and prospered in his hands."[1] I have in my own possession a copy of a tiny book called *Canons and Institutions*. It was published by an opponent of Fox and claimed to be a Quaker Discipline, drawn up and adopted by a large body of Friends from all parts of the Kingdom and assembled in "their new theatre in Gracechurch Street, London, in or about January 1668/9, George Fox being their president." This little thin book gathers up much of the organising work of the two years following the release from Scarborough. But the steps revealed in the surrepti-

[1] Quoted from Braithwaite's *Sec. Period of Quakerism*, p. 256.

tiously printed *Canons and Institutions* were only the beginning of the work. All the rest of Fox's life was to be spent in the patient task of developing and perfecting the organic system of the Society which he was slowly building throughout Great Britain and the Colonies and in overseeing and strengthening the practice of it.

Gifted as he was with the intuitions of a mystic and with the leadership of a prophet to his age and time, it can hardly be doubted, nevertheless, that his greatest service to the world was his creation of a permanent society, which was to transmit his spiritual contribution to coming generations, and which was with time to expand and develop the original seed-principle that had been committed to him. Fortunately he was conscious of the dangers that beset all elaborately constructed schemes and all big organisations, and his faith trusted naturally to those quiet life-forces and organic processes that operate inwardly in spiritual groups, and consequently he kept the machinery of his movement reduced to the lowest possible point and he raised vital processes to their highest potency. The Society, therefore, became a living body capable of growth and of frequent rejuvenescence.

Making, as he did, the meeting for worship the heart and centre of the Society which he formed, he prepared the way for a new type of group-mysticism. He sat on one occasion for hours in silence "to famish from words" the people who had thronged to hear him. In all his planning and arrangements he exalted the place of hush and silence, and he taught his followers to prize the times of quiet meditation in their gatherings for worship, so that he left behind him a fellowship of persons who knew how to cultivate the interior deeps within themselves and who had discovered how to make their own approach to God without external helps. His years of service were used not to make people dependent on him, but rather to ripen and prepare persons who were spiritually trained and inwardly skilled for personal communing with God and for joyous fellowship with Him. Wherever the Quaker meeting assembled, in the spirit and power of its primitive life, in city or country, in homeland or far-away colonies, there was a conscious sense of divine presence, a circulation of living currents of the Spirit, a breathing of a celestial atmosphere, a quickening of perception for calls of duty and the formation of inward tenderness toward all human need and suffering. Instead of producing a system that was an end in itself or that tended to supplant *the live idea* behind it, Fox was always endeavouring to leave a spiritual legacy which could be inherited only by persons who should themselves rewin it and freshly achieve it from generation to generation.

That was true, too, of the ideals embodied in the meetings for business. He did not fix a routine method which could be transmitted unchanged. He called his followers to a plan of democratic management of their affairs which could succeed and flourish only so long as the members themselves should keep in the currents of fresh life and should face up to and keep abreast of the growing tasks of a growing world. Once more it was a seed-germ and an organic principle which he supplied rather than a carefully constructed external system.

Fox's plan of gradated meetings with the application of ever wider group-wisdom for the guidance of the individual, was admirably fitted for a body which was at heart mystical. The solitary person left to follow a Light within himself might easily develop vagaries and might tend to mistake will-o'-the-wisps for celestial luminaries, as some of the early Quakers did do. Fox linked up the individual with a corporate fellowship and widened out the scope and tests of guidance. The Spirit of God revealed in and through the prophetic life and wisdom of a seasoned group was made superior to the insight or the impulse of a single person, and yet large provision was always made for safeguarding the spiritual rights and privileges of the person whose "heavenly vision" compelled him to say, "I cannot do otherwise." In these complicated and intricate matters no stage of perfection can be attained and no human contrivance can guarantee infallibility, but George Fox, called upon to fashion a working plan for a chaotic group, many of whom had been "Seekers" and "Familists" and "Ranters," extremely shy of restraint, produced a system solid enough to bring coherence and order and corporate strength, and at the same time malleable enough to allow for growth, expansion and fresh adjustment through the years, while scope was left free for the coming of new prophets and for the birth of fresh vision.

Loose and adjustable as was the proposed organisation, Fox nevertheless met a stubborn body of opposition to it, and the second formative stage of the Society resulted in a small "separation" led by two Johns—Wilkinson and Story—during the years 1675-78. It caused Fox much agony of spirit, as well as heavy labour, and it spread a dark cloud over what would otherwise have been fruitful years of spiritual harvest.

CHAPTER X

Marriage with Margaret Fell

IN 1669, on October 27th, George Fox and Margaret Fell of Swarthmore Hall were joined in marriage in Bristol. They had both for some time contemplated this union of their lives. Fox naïvely says that he "had received a commandment from the Lord for the accomplishment of it." There had for many years been a beautiful friendship between them. They were the two foremost guides of the Quaker movement, and together they planned the creative and constructive steps that won the convincements and eventually formed the Society which bound the scattered disciples into one body. Judge Fell had died in 1658, and after eleven years of widowhood Margaret accepted Fox's proposal of marriage, feeling, as he did, that it was "of the Lord."

He carefully took pains to see that none of the daughters of Judge Fell would lose anything financially by the marriage and that he himself should gain no profit out of the step. The seven daughters, three of whom at the time were married, gave their heartiest approval of the union and were throughout the life of Fox his most affectionate supporters and helpers. Four of the daughters, with the husbands of two of them, who were present at Bristol when the proposals of intentions were publicly made before Friends, declared their "free assent to the intended marriage" and further signified that they had "a sense that the thing intended to be accomplished doth stand in the Covenant of Light and Life," an ancient way of saying that it was "a marriage made in heaven." Fox himself had an exalted view of marriage and thought of it as a mystical and sacramental act. We have already seen that he endeavoured to restore marriage to the condition that existed in Eden, and to this end he called upon his friends to "come uppe Into ye marriage as it was in ye beginninge." There can be no doubt that he was dominated by this idea in his love-union with Margaret Fell and he wanted to have all other incentives eliminated before the step was taken. In May of this year,

[148]

Fox had gone, in company with four other "publishers of truth," on an extensive and strenuous religious journey through Ireland, and before setting out on this mission he had met Margaret Fell in London and had told her that he believed they should be married on his return to England, "for there was some Jumble in some mindes about it," [1] which means that Fox's friendship and fellowship with Mistress Fell had caused comment and gossip. He was back in England from the Irish visit in September, passing through a memorable storm at sea in which "the power of God went over the winds, He held them in His fists, His power bound them." He passed on, from Liverpool where he landed, to Bristol, where Margaret met him.

In one of the Bristol meetings just before the marriage took place, George Fox, according to the quaint account, "signified again his intention of marriage with Margaret Fell, to which he spoke largely in the power of the Lord and in His everlasting seed in which marriage was; but the life and power of the Lord was so over all that the words were not written, Friends being so filled and overcome with the

[1] *Cambridge Journal*, ii, p. 154.

power of the Lord." [1] The marriage itself took place in Broadmead Meeting House in Bristol. All seven of the Fell daughters were at the marriage and signed the certificate, as did also the husbands of the three who were married. In all, ninety-four Friends signed as witnesses. It was a time of exaltation, and George Fox himself was on one occasion during this high-tide experience carried almost to the state of ecstasy —"he could not tell whether he had a body or not a body."

But the wedding once over, "the publisher of truth" was again immediately off on his travels. The Quaker Act of 1662 and the two Conventicle Acts—the first in 1664 and the second in 1670—added tremendously to his labours and burdens and agonies. These acts let loose a pitiless havoc of persecution and suffering, and Fox stood in the forefront of the storm and danger throughout these dreadful years. With the prisons filling up with his peaceful followers, and with his work of establishing Monthly Meetings, Fox had no chance to enjoy a quiet home with the family he loved. His wife's account of the situation is touching and

[1] Quoted from Brayshaw's *The Personality of George Fox*, p. 64.

pathetic. She wrote in her beautiful Testimony to his memory: "Though the Lord had provided an outward habitation for him, yet he was not willing to stay at it, because it was so remote and far from London, where his service most lay. And my concern for God and His holy, eternal Truth was then in the north where God had placed and set me, and likewise for the ordering and governing of my children and family; so that we were very willing, both of us, to live apart some years upon God's account and His Truth's service, and to deny ourselves of that comfort which we might have had in being together."

The result was that in the twenty-one years that Fox lived after his marriage, he spent hardly more than five years with his wife. Two years were spent in America, as we shall see, fourteen months in Worcester jail, three months on his journey to Holland and Germany, with a second visit of seven weeks, and a long illness at Stratford and Enfield in 1670-71. These drew heavily on his time and energy. The rest of his strength and time went to the work of his life's mission.

George Fox wrote many letters, in his travels, to his "Dear Heart," as he always called his

wife. These letters are quite unlike modern
love letters, expressed as they are in the religious phraseology of the seventeenth century,
but a deep affection breathes through them and
they reveal a genuine spiritual quality of grace
and goodness. I will give one specimen of the
long correspondence. This letter was written
from Barbados, January 6, 1672.

My Dear Heart, to whom is my love, and to all
the children, in the Seed of Life that changeth not
but is over all; blessed be the Lord for ever. I have
undergone great sufferings in my body and spirit,
beyond words; but the God of heaven be praised,
His Truth is over all. I am now well; and if the
Lord permit, within a few days I pass from Barbados towards Jamaica; and I think to stay but
little there. I desire that ye may all be kept free in
the Seed of Life, out of all cumbrances. Friends are
generally well. Remember me to Friends that in-
quire after me. So no more, but my love in the Seed
and Life that changeth not.

G. F.

In the second period of his life Fox had the
joy and fellowship of a new band of friends
and helpers who were convinced of the truth
of his religious principle and way of life. The
most famous of these later disciples was Wil-

liam Penn, who became a Quaker in 1667, just when it was peculiarly dangerous and opprobrious to walk that path of life. He was the son of Admiral Sir William Penn, born in 1644, when Fox was seeking for the Light. It was not Fox in the first instance who touched young Penn's heart and spoke to his condition. It was Thomas Loe of Oxford who first, when on a visit in Ireland, deeply moved the boy of twelve with his message and who later again, after Penn had been sent down from the University of Oxford in disgrace and was in charge of his father's estate in Ireland, carried the young courtier all the way over to "convincement." He had a severe period of opposition from his father, when the Admiral discovered that his son of immense promise was turning Quaker, but once young Penn's face was set to walk this way of the cross there was nothing on earth that could turn him from what seemed to him a revelation of the way of Light and Truth. He became a brother beloved and soul-companion to George Fox. He developed into a powerful minister of the gospel; he grew to be a master of style and surpassed all other Friends of the seventeenth century in his power of writing and, though sometimes loose in thinking, he produced in a truly beautiful form excellent interpretations of vital and spiritual religion. But his founding of Pennsylvania in 1682 and his "holy experiment" in government in that colony is his immortal contribution, not alone to the Quaker faith, but to public life and to human civilisation. He wrote the most perfect sketch of Fox's character and mission that any one has yet produced. It is usually printed as a Preface to the *Journal*.

Next in importance among the new "convincements" was that of Robert Barclay of Ury, in Scotland. Fox himself had visited Scotland in 1657 after extensive labours in Wales. "When I first set my horse's feet upon Scottish ground," Fox wrote in the *Journal*, "I felt the Seed of God to sparkle about me, like innumerable sparks of fire." [1] And truly the Seed of God was there waiting to be awakened into life, though as Fox discovered there was much ploughing of "briery, brambly soil" before the seed would produce a harvest. Alexander Jaffray, George Keith, and Colonel David Barclay, father of Robert, were the most notable figures of the early Scotch "Seed." David Barclay had fought by the side of Gustavus Adolphus at the

[1] *Journal*, i, p. 412.

battle of Lützen and he had sat in two of Cromwell's Parliaments, but when he became a Quaker and "came to own Truth openly" he was imprisoned in Edinburgh, and his son Robert was "convinced" by a visit to his father and John Swinton, who was a fellow-prisoner with the old colonel in the Tolbooth. This occurred in 1666, when Robert Barclay was eighteen. He had been brought up as a boy in the strictest Calvinist views and then had been sent to Paris to study in the Scots Theological College, where he acquired skill and facility in both French and Latin, and became familiar with the writings of the Church fathers and the great theologians of the Church. He was easily the foremost Quaker scholar of his time. Like Penn, he came under the spell of Fox's message and spirit, and the learned bowed to the unlearned. Barclay in his short life rendered many services to the movement which he joined as a youth, but his supreme contribution was his monumental work, *The Apology*,[1] which appeared first in Latin, in 1676, and two years later in English. It was recognised at once by

[1] The full title was: *Apology for the True Christian Divinity, as the same is held forth and preached by the People called in scorn Quakers.*

all who read it, both Quakers and their opponents, to be a work of the first importance, and it was to remain for two hundred years the standard interpretation of Quakerism.

Barclay was a man of saintly life and there was unusual depth to his religious experience. Whenever he speaks out of his own experience he speaks as a genuine spiritual expert. He was, however, trained in the schools of theology rather than in the humanistic-mystical movement of the Spiritual Reformers, under the influence of which George Fox discovered his principle and way of life. Great, therefore, as Barclay was in the range of his scholarship and in the depth of his experience, he approaches the Quaker idea and method from a different point of view from that of Fox and the early "Children of the Light," and he gave the Quaker movement a trend of direction which materially altered it in the unfoldings of history, while Barclay's training in the philosophy and psychology of Descartes made him more dualistic in his thinking than were the simpler and less sophisticated founders of the movement. It would seem, too, that he had come under the influence of the Quietist movement on the Continent while he was in Paris.

Isaac Penington was another notable figure in the group of leaders. He was "convinced" much earlier than the two leaders just named, coming into the Quaker circle in 1658. He was a man of great gifts and qualities and was a person of real distinction. He had been for years a "Seeker," when at a great General Meeting at Swannington in 1658, where he first heard George Fox, he became a happy finder. "I have met," he declared with joy— "I have met with my God, I have met with my Saviour, I have felt the healings fall upon my soul from under His wings."

Penington suffered heavily for his new-found faith and his testimony, but he brought to the despised and persecuted cause both prestige and spiritual power. He was one of the most profoundly mystical of all the Quaker leaders and he possessed a striking style of expression, when he was at his best, though it must be said that he is often vague, misty, and wordy, rather than focal and luminous in his insights.

Gulielma Springett, who became the wife of William Penn, his "constant and entire friend," was the beautiful and gifted stepdaughter of Isaac Penington.

Thomas Ellwood, a friend of the Peningtons and an ardent suitor for the hand of Guli Springett, threw in his lot with the Quakers in 1659 and met in his turn the fierce anger of his father, who stormed against him even more violently than did Sir William Penn against his son. Ellwood was not of as great calibre or spiritual qualities as were the other three leaders mentioned above, though he was a man of distinct importance and he rendered a large and unforgettable service to the Society of Friends. He edited and, in a certain sense, created *The Journal of George Fox*. Out of manuscript journals and travel diaries and documents and letters, often badly written and often almost illegible, Ellwood gave us the great biography which permanently preserves the life and character and the creative work of George Fox. Ellwood's autobiographical story in his Life is a vigorously written and vividly pictorial book. He was John Milton's secretary and he suggested to the poet the writing of *Paradise Regained*.

Princess Elizabeth, daughter of Frederick, Elector Palatine, and granddaughter of James I of England, never actually became a full-fledged Friend, but she was deeply impressed by the Quaker message and way of life and she was in intimate correspondence and warm fellowship with Fox, Penn, and Barclay, the last named being a distant cousin of the princess. During the visit of Fox to Holland and Germany in 1677, two of the women in the party of travellers visited Princess Elizabeth and carried her a letter from Fox, which drew forth this affectionate reply.

Dear Friend: I cannot but have a tender love to those that love the Lord Jesus Christ, and to whom it is given, not only to believe in Him, but also to suffer for Him; therefore your letter and your Friends' visit have been both very welcome to me. I shall follow their and your counsel as far as God will afford me light and unction; remaining your loving friend,

ELIZABETH.

She was at the time one of the most learned women in Europe and one of the best minds of her century. She was the intimate friend and correspondent of Descartes and she influenced the life and thought of that great philosopher. After Descartes' death she came under the influence of the French mystic, Jean de Labadie, and accepted the position of Protestant abbess of Herford in Westphalia. She was twice visited by Penn and Barclay, once before and once after the writing of her letter to Fox. She was, at the time of her death, in 1680, in heart and spirit in full sympathy with Friends—a lover, as she calls it, of "the True Light"—and in frequent correspondence with them, though she never severed her old religious connections which would have been difficult for her to do, and never made open confession of "convincement."

Two more, among the many that might be mentioned as widely influential leaders among the early Quakers, were George Whitehead, who outlived most of the other "publishers of truth," and Thomas Story, powerful preacher, rhapsodical poet, man of deep scientific interests, and life-long friend of William Penn.

CHAPTER XI

Fox's American Travels

THE Quaker "invasion" of America began in 1656 with the coming of two
Quaker women, Mary Fisher and Ann Austin,
to Massachusetts. They were expelled from the
Province without having any opportunity to
proclaim their message in public. The first real
founders of American Quakerism were the
eleven Quaker men and women who came over
in the ship *Woodhouse* in 1657. The "log" of
the captain, Robert Fowler, who steered their
ship, is a unique document of remarkable interest. This group of eleven Quaker Argonauts
planted the "Seed" of their Truth on Long Island, throughout the Rhode Island Colonies—
i.e. Newport and Providence—and in Salem,
Sandwich, and many other towns of the Ply-
mouth and Massachusetts Bay Colonies. They
and their successors were quickly met with a
furious persecution, under which four Quakers

were martyred and many were whipped, mutilated, and imprisoned. But the "Seed" grew and expanded in the face of opposition, until it became too powerful to be exterminated by force. It spread also simultaneously in Maryland and in Virginia, so that by 1670 there was a large fringe of Quaker settlements and meetings from Portsmouth in New Hampshire to Cape Hatteras in Virginia, except for bare regions along the Connecticut shore, and the coasts of New Jersey and Delaware, which were soon to have their turn.

That was the situation in the Colonies when George Fox, with a little band of helpers and companions, set out on an ambitious journey of propagation. His companions were William Edmundson, John Rous, John Stubbs, Thomas Briggs, Solomon Eccles, James Lancaster, John Cartwright, Robert Widders, George Pattison, John Hull, Elizabeth Miers, and his remarkable first convert, Elizabeth Hooton, who bore in her body the marks of her faith. The vessel, which was a yacht, was named the *Industry*, with Thomas Foster for captain, and carried about fifty passengers. There was already a small Quaker settlement in the island of Barbados and thither the party of Quakers were bound for their first objective.

The *Travel Diary* for the American journey is a vivid document and I shall let Fox tell his own story in his own words, reminding the reader in advance that the journey resulted in a very great expansion of Quakerism in the Colonies where it already existed, with a further extension of it into the Carolinas, and eventually led to the purchase and settlement of New Jersey and to the launching of "the Holy Experiment" in Pennsylvania. There is an almost Homeric simplicity to this *Travel Diary*. It reveals a swiftness of movement and a sincerity of purpose, as well as a rare and touching faith in God and in the fundamental nature of man. It will be given with many abbreviations and omissions, as follows:

"In the afternoon [August 13, 1671] the wind serving, I took leave of my wife and other Friends, and went on board. Before we could sail, there being two of the King's frigates riding in the Downs, the captain of one of them sent his press-master on board us, who took three of our seamen. This would certainly have delayed, if not wholly prevented, our voyage, had not the captain of the other frigate, being

[163]

informed of the leakiness of our vessel, and the length of our voyage, in compassion and much civility, spared us two of his own men.

"Being clear, we set sail in the evening, and next morning overtook part of that fleet about the height of Dover. We soon reached the rest, and in a little time left them all behind; for our yacht was counted a very swift sailer. But she was very leaky, so that the seamen and some of the passengers, did, for the most part, pump day and night. One day they observed that in two hours' time she sucked in sixteen inches of water in the well.

"When we had been about three weeks at sea, one afternoon we spied a vessel about four leagues astern of us. Our master said it was a Sallee [1] man-of-war, that seemed to give us chase. He said, 'Come let us go to supper, and when it grows dark we shall lose him.' This he spoke to please and pacify the passengers, some of whom began to be very apprehensive of the danger. But Friends were well satisfied in them-

[1] A Moorish pirate ship, named from Sallee, a seaport of Morocco. This incident not only indicates Fox's simple faith in God, but it also is a good illustration of the way in which he inspired confidence in others. The captain believes in him.

selves, having faith in God, and no fear upon their spirits.

"When the sun was gone down, I saw out of my cabin the ship making towards us. When it grew dark, we altered our course to miss her; but she altered also, and gained upon us.

"At night the master and others came into my cabin, and asked me what they should do. I told them I was no mariner; and I asked them what they thought was best to do. They said there were but two ways, either to outrun him, or to tack about, and hold the same course we were going before. I told them that if he were a thief, they might be sure he would tack about too; and as for outrunning him, it was to no purpose to talk of that, for they saw he sailed faster than we. They asked me again what they should do, 'for,' they said, 'if the mariners had taken Paul's counsel, they had not come to the damage they did.' I answered that it was a trial of faith, and therefore the Lord was to be waited on for counsel.

"So, retiring in spirit, the Lord showed me that His life and power were placed between us and the ship that pursued us. I told this to the master and the rest, and that the best way was to tack about and steer our right course.

I desired them also to put out all their candles but the one they steered by, and to speak to all the passengers to be still and quiet.

"About eleven at night the watch called and said they were just upon us. This disquieted some of the passengers. I sat up in my cabin, and, looking through the porthole, the moon being not quite down, I saw them very near us. I was getting up to go out of the cabin; but remembering the word of the Lord, that His life and power were placed between us and them, I lay down again.

"The master and some of the seamen came again, and asked me if they might not steer such a point. I told them they might do as they would.

"By this time the moon was quite down. A fresh gale arose, and the Lord hid us from them; we sailed briskly on and saw them no more.

"The next day, being the first day of the week [Sunday], we had a public meeting in the ship, as we usually had on that day throughout the voyage, and the Lord's presence was greatly among us. I desired the people to remember the mercies of the Lord, who had delivered them; for they might have been all in the

Turks' hands by that time, had not the Lord's hand saved them.

"Having been three months or more in Barbados, and having visited Friends, thoroughly settled meetings, and despatched the service for which the Lord brought me thither, I felt my spirit clear of that island, and found drawings to Jamaica. When I had communicated this to Friends, I acquainted the Governor also, and divers of his council, that I intended shortly to leave the island, and go to Jamaica. This I did that, as my coming thither was open and public, so my departure also might be.

"I set sail from Barbados to Jamaica on the 8th of the Eleventh month, 1671; Robert Widders, William Edmundson, Solomon Eccles and Elizabeth Hooton going with me. Thomas Briggs and John Stubbs remained in Barbados, with whom were John Rous and William Bailey.

"We had a quick and easy passage to Jamaica, where we met again with our Friends James Lancaster, John Cartwright, and George Pattison, who had been labouring there in the service of Truth; into which we forthwith entered with them, travelling up and down through the island, which is large; and a brave country it is, though the people are, many of them, debauched and wicked.

"We had much service. There was a great convincement, and many received the Truth, some of whom were people of account in the world. We had many meetings there, which were large, and very quiet. The people were civil to us, so that not a mouth was opened against us. I was twice with the Governor, and some other magistrates, who all carried themselves kindly towards me.

"About a week after we landed in Jamaica, Elizabeth Hooton, a woman of great age, who had travelled much in Truth's service, and suffered much for it, departed this life. She was well the day before she died, and departed in peace, like a lamb, bearing testimony to Truth at her departure.

"When we had been about seven weeks in Jamaica, had brought Friends into pretty good order, and settled several meetings amongst them, we left Solomon Eccles there; the rest of us embarked for Maryland, leaving Friends and Truth prosperous in Jamaica, the Lord's power being over all, and His blessed Seed reigning.

"We went on board on the 8th of First month

1671,[1] and, having contrary winds, were a full week sailing forwards and backwards before we could get out of sight of Jamaica.

"A difficult voyage this proved, and dangerous, especially in passing through the Gulf of Florida, where we met with many trials by winds and storms.

"But the great God, who is Lord of the sea and land, and who rideth upon the wings of the wind, did by His power preserve us through many and great dangers, when by extreme stress of weather our vessel was many times likely to be upset, and much of her tackling broken. And indeed we were sensible that the Lord was a God at hand, and that His ear was open to the supplications of His people.

"For when the winds were so strong and boisterous, and the storms and tempests so great that the sailors knew not what to do, but let the ship go which way she would, then did we pray unto the Lord, who graciously heard us, calmed the winds and the seas, gave us seasonable weather, and made us to rejoice in His salvation.

"We were between six and seven weeks in this passage from Jamaica to Maryland. Some days before we came to land, after we had en-

[1] March 8, 1672. According to modern calendar.

tered the bay of Patuxent River, a great storm
arose, which cast a boat upon us for shelter, in
which were several people of account in the
world. We took them in; but the boat was lost,
with five hundred pounds' worth of goods in
it, as they said. They continued on board several days, not having any means to get off;
and we had a very good meeting with them in
the ship.

"But provisions grew short, for they brought
none in with them; and ours, by reason of the
length of our voyage, were well-nigh spent
when they came to us; so that with their living
with us too, we had now little or none left.
Whereupon George Pattison took a boat, and
ventured his life to get to shore; the hazard
was so great that all but Friends concluded he
would be cast away. Yet it pleased the Lord
to bring him safe to land, and in a short time
after the Friends of the place came to fetch
us to land also, in a seasonable time, for our
provisions were quite spent.

"We partook also of another great deliver-
ance in this voyage, through the good providence of the Lord which we came to understand
afterwards. For when we were determined to
come from Jamaica, we had our choice of two

vessels, that were both bound for the same coast. One of these was a frigate, the other a yacht. The master of the frigate, we thought, asked unreasonably for our passage, which made us agree with the master of the yacht, who offered to carry us ten shilling apiece cheaper than the other.

"We went on board the yacht, and the frigate came out together with us, intending to be consorts during the voyage. For several days we sailed together; but, with calms and contrary winds, we were soon separated. After that the frigate, losing her way, fell among the Spaniards, by whom she was taken and plundered, and the master and mate made prisoners. Afterwards, being retaken by the English, she was sent home to her owners in Virginia. When we came to understand this we saw and admired the providence of God, who preserved us out of our enemies' hands; and he that was covetous fell among the covetous.

"Here we found John Burnyeat, intending shortly to sail for England; but on our arrival he altered his purpose, and joined us in the Lord's service. He had appointed a general meeting for all the Friends in the province of Maryland, that he might see them together, and take his leave of them before he departed out of the country. It was so ordered by the good providence of God that we landed just in time to reach that meeting, by which means we had a very seasonable opportunity of taking the Friends of the province together.

"A very large meeting this was, and it held four days, to which, besides Friends, came many other people, several of whom were of considerable quality in the world's account. There were five or six justices of the peace, the speaker of their assembly, one of their council, and others of note, who seemed well satisfied with the meeting. After the public meetings were over, the men's and women's meetings began, wherein I opened to Friends the service thereof, to their great satisfaction.

"After this we went to the Cliffs, where another general meeting was appointed. We went some of the way by land, the rest by water, and, a storm arising, our boat was run aground, in danger of being beaten to pieces, and the water came in upon us. I was in a great sweat, having come very hot out of a meeting before, and now was wet with the water besides; yet, having faith in the divine power, I was preserved from taking hurt, blessed be the Lord!

"To this meeting came many who received the Truth with reverence. We had also a men's meeting and a women's meeting. Most of the backsliders came in again; and several meetings were established for taking care of the affairs of the Church.

"After these two general meetings, we parted company, dividing ourselves unto several coasts, for the service of Truth. James Lancaster and John Cartwright went by sea for New England; William Edmundson and three Friends more sailed for Virginia, where things were much out of order; John Burnycat, Robert Widders, George Pattison, and I, with several Friends of the province, went over by boat to the Eastern Shore,[1] and had a meeting there on the First-day.

"There many people received the Truth with gladness, and Friends were greatly refreshed. A very large and heavenly meeting it was. Several persons of quality in that country were at it, two of whom were justices of the peace. It was upon me from the Lord to send to the Indian emperor and his kings to come to that meeting. The emperor came and was at the meeting. His kings, lying further off, could not reach

[1] Eastern shore of Chesapeake Bay.

the place in time. Yet they came soon after, with their cockarooses.[1]

"I had in the evening two good opportunities with them; they heard the word of the Lord willingly, and confessed to it. What I spoke to them I desired them to speak to their people, and to let them know that God was raising up His standard and glorious ensign of righteousness. They carried themselves very courteously and lovingly, and inquired where the next meeting would be, saying that they would come to it. Yet they said they had had a great debate with their council about their coming, before they came.

"The next day we began our journey by land to New England; a tedious journey through the woods and wilderness, over bogs and great rivers.

"We took horse at the head of Tredhaven creek, and travelled through the woods till we came a little above the head of Miles river, by which we passed, and rode to the head of Wye river, and so to the head of Chester river, where, making a fire, we took up our lodging in the woods. Next morning we travelled the woods till we came to Sassafras river, which we went

[1] Local word for Indian chief or headman.

over in canoes, causing our horses to swim beside us.

"Then we rode to Bohemia river, where, in like manner swimming our horses, we ourselves went over in canoes. We rested a little at a plantation by the way, but not long, for we had thirty miles to ride that afternoon if we would reach a town, which we were willing to do, and therefore rode hard for it. I, with some others, whose horses were strong, got to the town that night, exceedingly tired, and wet to the skin; but George Pattison and Robert Widders, being weaker-horsed, were obliged to lie in the woods that night also.

"The town we went to was a Dutch town, called New Castle,[1] whither Robert Widders and George Pattison came to us next morning.

"We departed thence, and got over the river Delaware, not without great danger of some of our lives. When we were over we were troubled to procure guides, which were hard to get, and very chargeable. Then had we that wilderness country, since called West Jersey, to pass through, not then inhabited by English; so that we sometimes travelled a whole day together without seeing man or woman, house or dwell-

[1] In Delaware.

[175]

ing-place. Sometimes we lay in the woods by a fire, and sometimes in the Indians' wigwams or houses.

"We came one night to an Indian town, and lay at the house of the king, who was a very pretty [1] man. Both he and his wife received us very lovingly, and his attendants (such as they were) were very respectful to us. They gave us mats to lie on; but provision was very short with them, they having caught but little that day. At another Indian town where we stayed the king came to us, and he could speak some English. I spoke to him much, and also to his people; and they were very loving to us.

"At length we came to Middletown, an English plantation in East Jersey, and there we found some Friends; but we could not stay to have a meeting at that time, being earnestly pressed in our spirits to get to the half-year's meeting of Friends at Oyster Bay, in Long Island, which was very near at hand.

"We went with a Friend, Richard Hartshorn, brother of Hugh Hartshorn, the upholsterer, in London, who received us gladly at his house, where we refreshed ourselves; and then he carried us and our horses in his own boat over a

[1] That is, kindly-spirited.

great water, which occupied most part of the day getting over, and set us upon Long Island. We got that evening to Friends at Gravesend, with whom we tarried that night, and next day got to Flushing, and the day following reached Oyster Bay; several Friends of Gravesend and Flushing accompanied us.

"The half-year's meeting began next day, which was the first day of the week, and lasted four days. The first and second days we had public meetings for worship, to which people of all sorts came; on the third day were the men's and women's meetings, wherein the affairs of the Church were taken care of.

"After Friends were gone to their several habitations, we stayed some days upon the island; had meetings in several parts thereof, and good service for the Lord. When we were clear of the island, we returned to Oyster Bay, waiting for a wind to carry us to Rhode Island, which was computed to be about two hundred miles. As soon as the wind served, we set sail. We arrived there on the thirtieth day of the Third month, and were gladly received by Friends. We went to the house of Nicholas Easton, who at that time was governor of the island; where we rested, being very weary with travelling.

"On First-day following we had a large meeting, to which came the deputy-governor and several justices, who were mightily affected with the Truth. The week following, the Yearly Meeting for all the Friends of New England and the other colonies adjacent, was held in this island, to which, besides very many Friends who lived in those parts, came John Stubbs from Barbados, and James Lancaster and John Cartwright from another way.

"This meeting lasted six days, the first four days being general public meetings for worship, to which abundance of other people came; for they having no priest in the island, and so no restriction to any particular way of worship; and both the governor and deputy-governor, with several justices of the peace, daily frequenting the meetings; this so encouraged the people that they flocked in from all parts of the island. Very good service we had amongst them, and Truth had good reception.

"I have rarely observed a people, in the state wherein they stood, to hear with more attention, diligence, and affection, than generally they did, during the four days; which was also taken notice of by other Friends.

"These public meetings over, the men's meeting began, which was large, precious, and weighty. The day following was the women's meeting, which also was large and very solemn.

"These two meetings being for ordering the affairs of the Church, many weighty things were opened, and communicated to them, by way of advice, information, and instruction in the services relating thereunto; that all might be kept clean, sweet and savoury amongst them. In these, several men's and women's meetings for other parts were agreed and settled, to take care of the poor, and other affairs of the Church, and to see that all who profess Truth walk according to the glorious gospel of God.

"When this great general meeting was ended, it was somewhat hard for Friends to part; for the glorious power of the Lord, which was over all, and His blessed Truth and life flowing amongst them, had so knit and united them together, that they spent two days in taking leave one of another, and of the Friends of the island; and then, being mightily filled with the presence and power of the Lord, they went away with joyful hearts to their several habitations, in the several colonies where they lived.

"When Friends had taken their leave one of another, we, who travelled amongst them, dispersed ourselves into our several services, as the Lord ordered us.

"Then we had a meeting at Providence [Roger Williams's Colony] which was very large, consisting of many sorts of people. I had a great travail upon my spirit, that it might be preserved quiet, and that Truth might be brought over the people, might gain entrance, and have a place in them; for they were generally above the priest in high notions; and some of them came on purpose to dispute. But the Lord, whom we waited upon, was with us, and His power went over them all; and His blessed Seed was exalted and set above all. The disputers were silent, and the meeting was quiet and ended well; praised be the Lord! The people went away mightily satisfied, much desiring another meeting.

"This place (called Providence) was about thirty miles from Rhode Island [*i.e.*, Newport]; and we went to it by water. The Governor of Rhode Island, and many others, went with me thither; and we had the meeting in a

[180]

great barn, which was thronged with people, so that I was exceedingly hot, and in a great sweat; but all was well; the glorious power of the Lord shone over all; glory to the great God for ever!

"We got safe to Oyster Bay, in Long Island, which, they say, is about two hundred miles from Rhode Island, the seventh of the Sixth month, very early in the morning.

"At Oyster Bay we had a very large meeting. The same day James Lancaster and Christopher Holder went over the bay to Rye, on the continent, in Governor Winthrop's government [Connecticut], and had a meeting there.

"From Oyster Bay, we passed about thirty miles to Flushing, where we had a very large meeting, many hundreds of people being there; some of whom came about thirty miles to it. A glorious and heavenly meeting it was (praised be the Lord God!), and the people were much satisfied.

"Meanwhile Christopher Holder and some other Friends went to a town in Long Island, called Jamaica, and had a meeting there.

"We passed from Flushing to Gravesend, about twenty miles, and there had three precious meetings; to which many would have come from New York, but that the weather hindered them.

"Being clear of this place, we hired a sloop, and, the wind serving, set out for the new country now called Jersey. Passing down the bay by Coney Island, Natton Island,[1] and Staten Island, we came to Richard Hartshorn's at Middletown harbour,[2] about break of day, the twenty-seventh of the Sixth month.

"Next day we rode about thirty miles into that country, through the woods, and over very bad bogs, one worse than all the rest; the descent into which was so steep that we were fain to slide down with our horses, and then let them lie and breathe themselves before they could go on. This place the people of the country called Purgatory.

"We got at length to Shrewsbury, in East Jersey, and on First-day had a precious meeting there, to which Friends and other people came from afar, and the blessed presence of the Lord was with us. The same week we had a men's and women's meeting out of most parts of New Jersey.

"They are building a meeting place in the midst of them and there is a monthly and gen-

[1] Now Governor's Island.   [2] In New Jersey.

eral meeting set up which will be of great service in those parts in keeping up the gospel order and government of Christ Jesus, of the increase of which there is no end, that they who are faithful may see that all who profess the holy Truth live in the pure religion, and walk as becometh the gospel.

"While we were at Shrewsbury, an accident befell, which for the time was a great exercise to us. John Jay, a Friend of Barbados, who had come with us from Rhode Island, and intended to accompany us through the woods to Maryland, being to try a horse, got upon his back, and the horse fell a-running, cast him down upon his head, and broke his neck, as the people said. Those that were near him took him up as dead, carried him a good way, and laid him on a tree.

"I got to him as soon as I could; and, feeling him, concluded he was dead. As I stood pitying him and his family, I took hold of his hair, and his head turned any way, his neck was so limber. Whereupon I took his head in both my hands, and, setting my knees against the tree, I raised his head, and perceived there was nothing out or broken that way.

"Then I put one hand under his chin, and

the other behind his head, and raised his head two or three times with all my strength, and brought it in. I soon perceived his neck began to grow stiff again, and then he began to rattle in his throat, and quickly after to breathe.

"The people were amazed; but I bade them have a good heart, be of good faith, and carry him into the house. They did so, and set him by the fire. I bade them get him something warm to drink, and put him to bed. After he had been in the house a while he began to speak; but did not know where he had been.

"The next day we passed away (and he with us, pretty well) about sixteen miles to a meeting at Middletown, through woods and bogs, and over a river; where we swam our horses, and got over ourselves upon a hollow tree. Many hundred miles did he travel with us after this.[1]

"To this meeting came most of the people of the town. A glorious meeting we had, and

[1] This narrative has sometimes been questioned and sometimes been taken to prove that Fox was an instrument in working miracles. Neither solution is satisfactory, or necessary. Recent medical annals give similar cases. A dislocated neck is not necessarily fatal. The incident shows again Fox's readiness in dealing coolly and skilfully with hard situations. He endeavours to do what *can* be done.

the Truth was over all; blessed be the great Lord God for ever! After the meeting we went to Middletown Harbor, about five miles, in order to take our long journey next morning, through the woods towards Maryland; having hired Indians for our guides.

"I determined to pass through the woods on the other side of Delaware bay, that we might head the creeks and rivers as much as possible. On the 9th of the Seventh month we set forwards, and passed through many Indian towns, and over some rivers and bogs; and when we had ridden about forty miles, we made a fire at night, and lay down by it. As we came among the Indians, we declared the day of the Lord to them.

"Next day we travelled fifty miles, as we computed; and at night, finding an old house, which the Indians had forced the people to leave, we made a fire and stayed there, at the head of Delaware Bay.

"Next day we swam our horses over a river about a mile wide, first to an island called Upper Tinicum, and then to the mainland; having hired Indians to help us over in their canoes. This day we rode but about thirty miles, and came at night to a Swede's house, where we got a little straw, and stayed that night.

"Next day, having hired another guide, we travelled about forty miles through the woods, and made a fire at night, by which we lay, and dried ourselves; for we were often wet in our travels.

"The next day we passed over a desperate river,[1] which had in it many rocks and broad stones, very hazardous to us and our horses. Thence we came to Christiana River, where we swam over our horses, and went over ourselves in canoes; but the sides of this river were so bad and miry, that some of the horses were almost laid up.

"Thence we came to New Castle,[2] heretofore called New Amsterdam; and being very weary, and inquiring in the town where we

[1] The "desperate river" was probably the Brandywine, and the Christiana "River" is Christiana Creek, formed from a junction of Red Clay and White Clay Creeks. It finds the Delaware about two miles below Wilmington. The Bohemia and Sassafras Rivers are two of the many arms of Chesapeake Bay. The "Kentish Shore" is the shore of Kent County, Maryland. Tredhaven (or Thirdhaven) is farther down the bay, where the boats were so thick it seemed like the Thames! A meeting was established here which remains until the present time.

[2] In Delaware.

might buy some corn for our horses, the governor came and invited me to his house, and afterwards desired me to lodge there; telling me he had a bed for me, and I should be welcome. So I stayed, the other Friends being taken care of also.

"This was on a Seventh-day; and he offered his house for a meeting, we had the next day a pretty large one; for most of the town were at it. Here had never been a meeting before, nor any within a great way; but this was a very precious one. Many were tender, and confessed to the Truth, and some received it; blessed be the Lord for ever!

"The 16th of the Seventh month we set forward, and travelled, as near as we could compute, about fifty miles, through the woods and over the bogs, heading Bohemia River and Sassafras River. At night we made a fire in the woods, and lay there all night. It being rainy weather, we got under some thick trees for shelter, and afterwards dried ourselves again by the fire.

"Next day we waded through Chester River, a very broad water, and afterwards passing through many bad bogs, lay that night also in the woods by a fire, not having gone above thirty miles that day. The day following we travelled hard, though we had some troublesome bogs in our way; we rode about fifty miles, and got safe that night to Robert Harwood's at Miles River,[1] in Maryland.

"This was the 18th of the Seventh month; and though we were very weary, and much dirtied with the bogs, yet hearing of a meeting next day, we went to it, and from it to John Edmundson's. Thence we went three or four miles by water to a meeting on the First-day following.

"At this meeting a judge's wife, who had never been at any of our meetings, was reached. She said after the meeting that she would rather hear us once than the priests a thousand times. Many others also were well satisfied; for the power of the Lord was eminently with us. Blessed for ever be His holy name!

"We passed thence about twenty-two miles, and had a good meeting upon the Kentish shore, to which one of the judges came. After another good meeting hard-by, at William Wilcock's, where we had good service for the Lord, we went by water about twenty miles to a very large meeting, where were some hundreds of

[1] Now St. Michael's.

people, four justices of peace, the high sheriff of Delaware, and others. There were also an Indian emperor or governor, and two others of the chief men among the Indians.

"With these Indians I had a good opportunity. I spoke to them by an interpreter: they heard the Truth attentively, and were very loving. A blessed meeting this was, of great service both for convincing and for establishing in the Truth those that were convinced of it. Blessed be the Lord, who causeth His blessed Truth to spread!

"After the meeting there came to me a woman whose husband was one of the judges of that country, and a member of the assembly there. She told me that her husband was sick, not likely to live; and desired me to go home with her to see him. It was three miles to her house, and I being just come hot out of the meeting, it was hard for me then to go; yet considering the service, I got a horse, went with her, visited her husband, and spoke to him what the Lord gave me. The man was much refreshed, and finely raised up by the power of the Lord; and afterwards came to our meetings.

"I went back to the Friends that night, and next day we departed thence about nineteen or twenty miles to Tredhaven creek, to John Edmundson's again; whence, the 3d of Eighth month, we went to the General Meeting for all Maryland Friends.[1]

"This held five days. The first three meetings were for public worship, to which people of all sorts came; the other two were men's and women's meetings. To the public meetings came many Protestants of divers sorts, and some Papists. Amongst these were several magistrates and their wives, and other persons of chief account in the country. There were so many besides Friends that it was thought there were sometimes a thousand people at one of these meetings; so that, though they had not long before enlarged their meeting-place, and made it as large again as it was before, it could not contain the people.

"I went by boat every day four or five miles to it, and there were so many boats at that time passing upon the river that it was almost like the Thames. The people said there were never so many boats seen there together before, and one of the justices said he had never seen so many people together in that country before.

[1] What is now called Baltimore Yearly Meeting was established in 1672.

It was a very heavenly meeting, wherein the presence of the Lord was gloriously manifested. Friends were sweetly refreshed, the people generally satisfied, and many convinced; for the blessed power of the Lord was over all; everlasting praises to His holy name for ever!

"After the public meetings were over, the men's and women's meetings began, and were held the other two days; for I had something to impart to them which concerned the glory of God, the order of the gospel, and the government of Christ Jesus.

When these meetings were over, we took our leave of Friends in those parts, whom we left well established in the Truth."

The *Travel Diary* proceeds to narrate more service in Maryland, "in foul weather and much rain," but with peace in the travellers' hearts, and with powerful meetings among responsive people. Then follows an account of a difficult but momentous journey through the Colony of Virginia and into the Carolinas, where much new ground was broken for the Quaker "Seed." The return journey to Maryland was a hard and wearying one, but it bore good fruit. When he had covered the field of his extensive labours in the southern Colonies, Fox set himself to finish his work of organisation preparatory to his return to England. Never anywhere in the world had his efforts been more effective.

"Having travelled through most parts of the country," he wrote, "and visited most of the plantations, and having sounded the alarm to all people where we came, and proclaimed the day of God's salvation amongst them, we found our spirits began to be clear of these parts of the world, and to draw towards Old England again.

"We took our leave of Friends, parting in great tenderness, in the sense of the heavenly life and virtuous power of the Lord that was livingly felt amongst us; and went by water to the place where we were to take shipping, many Friends accompanying us thither and tarrying with us that night.

"Next day, the 21st of the Third month [May], 1673, we set sail for England; the same day Richard Covell came on board our ship, having had his own taken from him by the Dutch.

"We had foul weather and contrary winds, which caused us to cast anchor often, so that we were till the 31st ere we could get past the capes of Virginia and out into the main sea. But after this we made good speed, and on the 28th of the Fourth month [June] cast anchor at King's Road, which is the harbour for Bristol.

"We had on our passage very high winds and tempestuous weather, which made the sea exceedingly rough, the waves rising like mountains; so that the masters and sailors wondered at it, and said they had never seen the like before. But though the wind was strong it set for the most part with us, so that we sailed before it; and the great God who commands the winds, who is Lord of heaven, of earth, and the seas, and whose wonders are seen in the deep, steered our course and preserved us from many imminent dangers. The same good hand of Providence that went with us, and carried us safely over, watched over us in our return, and brought us safely back again; thanksgiving and praises be to his holy name for ever!

"Many sweet and precious meetings we had on board the ship during this voyage (commonly two a week) wherein the blessed presence of the Lord did greatly refresh us, and often break in upon and tender the company.

"When we came into Bristol harbour, there lay a man-of-war, and the press-master came on board to impress our men. We had a meeting at that time in the ship with the seamen, before we went to shore, and the press-master sat down with us, stayed the meeting, and was well satisfied with it. After the meeting, I spoke to him to leave in our ship two of the men he had impressed, for he had impressed four, one of whom was a lame man. He said, 'At your request I will.'

"We went on shore that afternoon, and got to Shirehampton. We procured horses and rode to Bristol that night, where Friends received us with great joy."

CHAPTER XII

Social Work

IN SPITE of the fact that George Fox was a mystic and that he laid so much stress on the inward way, he was nevertheless of all things a man of action and concerned with the practical tasks of life. His religion was fully as much outward as it was inward. His Divine Light was a principle of unity. It bound into one whole the two diverse attitudes of his nature, and he was following his bent alike when he sat on a haystack unmoved for three hours in silence and when he rode through the English counties, or the American forests, preaching and creating meetings. From the first his religion took a practical turn. He did not think of religion primarily as a way to win a peaceful refuge in the world beyond. Having dropped his burdens of theology as Bunyan did his burden of sin, he lost at the same time the habit of considering salvation as a title to a mansion in heaven. It became for him at once a way of living in the world now, a program for the actual pilgrimage we are engaged in. Fox seldom uses the word through which Christ expressed his central program—the kingdom of God—but in a rough and general way its ideals are his ideals. He wanted to see God's will done on earth, where conditions are difficult, as it is now done in heaven, where conditions are easy. One of Fox's apostolic men, Francis Howgill, bears this fine testimony: "We often said to one another, with great joy of heart, 'What! Is the kingdom of God come to be with men?' "

For the present age the most important thing about Fox's mission in the world is not his theory, but his practical way of life. Truth for him was always something a man can not only think but *be*. To discover a truth involves the apostolic task of going out and doing it. Fox, like St. Francis and like their greater Master of Galilee, believed absolutely in the conquering power of faith and love. Swinging away as he did from the prevailing theories of human depravity, he went far over to the other extreme and took a strikingly optimistic view of man. His most frequent phrase is, "Mind that of God in every man." Set man free from tyranny and oppression, liberate him from false theories of life, draw out his potential capacities by a true education, awaken him to a consciousness of God within him, and there are no limits to his spiritual possibilities. The one great method of ending the old way of life and inaugurating the new is the practice of love. Act with honesty and sincerity under all circumstances, meet everybody with an understanding mind as well as with trust and confidence, reveal a spirit of spontaneous and unfeigned love, and there will prove to be pretty nearly nothing in the world that will successfully resist that impact.

Notwithstanding the fact of his early years of solitude and withdrawal, Fox was by disposition a social-minded man. He *saw* and *felt* wrong social conditions as unerringly as he saw and felt the nearness of God. Before he had even set forth to preach his message of the Light he had an impression that he ought to go to the justices and tell them to consider the condition of servants and to see to it that these servants had fair wages. "At a certain time, when I was at Mansfield, there was a sitting of the justices about hiring of servants; and it was upon me from the Lord to go and speak to the justices, that they should not oppress the servants in their wages. So I walked towards the inn where they sat; but finding a company of fiddlers there, I did not go in, but thought to come in the morning, when I might have a more serious opportunity to discourse with them. But when I came in the morning, they were gone, and I was struck even blind, that I could not see. I inquired of the innkeeper where the justices were to sit that day; and he told me, at a town eight miles off. My sight began to come to me again; and I went and ran thitherward as fast as I could. When I was come to the house where they were, and many servants with them, I exhorted the justices not to oppress the servants in their wages, but to do that which was right and just to them; and I exhorted the servants to do their duties, and serve honestly. They all received my exhortation kindly; for I was moved of the Lord therein." [1]

He was always concerned for toilers. He was deeply distressed by the excessive drinking in taverns. He was shocked as soon as he saw the way men and women lived in jails and prisons. He was convinced that the prisons where people were supposed to be "corrected" were inhuman instruments. He knew that capital

[1] *Journal*, i, p. 27.

punishment was wrong. He was certain that the entire method of correction was on the wrong basis and defeated itself. "As I walked towards the jail, the word of the Lord came to me, saying, 'My love was always to thee, and thou art in my love.' And I was ravished with the sense of the love of God, and greatly strengthened in my inward man. But when I came into the jail where those prisoners were, a great power of darkness struck at me; and I sat still, having my spirit gathered into the love of God." [1]

He saw in Negroes and North American Indians, in the unfavoured races everywhere, moral and spiritual possibilities which others had hardly suspected. He had an unlimited faith in education and he was an unceasing advocate of it. He wanted boys and girls to study "everything civil and useful in the creation." It is useless to expect that he would by miraculous insight have the sound principles of sociology which our scientific age is slowly building up. The important fact is that again and again he rightly diagnosed the trouble and put his finger on the diseased spot. With a swift intuition he pronounced against evil customs which had gone unchallenged for centuries, and with the same

[1] *Ibid.*, i, p. 47.

sure insight he suggested a new way of action. He had, as I have said, a great stock of trust and confidence in man. His foundation theory of man, as a being possessed of something of God, taught from within by direct illumination, made him hopeful and persistently expectant.

Even his most odd and bizarre convictions and peculiarities had reference to his passion for a better social order and for a truer relationship. The use of "thee" and "thou" had its origin with him in a determination to treat all men alike. It was a badge of human equality. He would not say "thou" to the laborer and "you" to the magnate. As in his boyhood use of "verily," so here, he proposed to make language a medium of truth and sincerity. His lips should utter only what his heart and mind endorsed. If formal etiquette expected him to say to a man what he very well knew was not true, then he resolved to have nothing more to do with formal etiquette till the end of the world! Some of his points of social reform are trivial and hair-splitting, no doubt. He sometimes makes a mountain out of an ant-hill. But his basic principle was a high and significant one. Truth and sincerity were the two guardian angels who attended Fox's steps. He was a fallible man, like the rest of us, and he was not always wise, but this can be said: he minded the Light in his soul and he *did* what he dared to dream of.

He attacked the most gigantic problems in the same spirit in which men have since set forth to conquer the poles of the earth or to climb Mt. Everest. He had a dash of that same divine folly which was raised to such a height in "God's little fool" of Assisi. He took quite literally the saying that there are no mountains which can successfully resist a well-grounded faith. War had always existed. It was as old as fear and hate. It was due to the thrust of immemorial instincts. And men said then, as was said two thousand years before, "What has been is what shall be." No, said Fox, war is wrong; it is immoral, it is inhuman and it shall not be. There is a spirit which conquers it and abolishes it, and I propose to incarnate that spirit and to practise it and to call others to that way of life until we girdle the world with men and women who live in "that life and power which does away with the occasion for all war!" [1] "The seed of God reigns, and is atop of the Devil and all his works" is one of

[1] *Journal*, i, p. 68.

his great phrases. "I told them I knew whence all wars arose, even from the lusts, according to James's doctrine; and that I lived in the virtue of that life and power that took away the occasion of all wars. Yet they courted me to accept of their offer, and thought I did but compliment them. But I told them I was come into the covenant of peace which was before wars and strifes were." [1] Again people said, "What has been done is what shall be done." But once more this simple knight of God rode forth with no other strength than his faith that *what is eternally right can in the end be done.* He did not live to see the new world which his faith forecast. We do not altogether see it yet, after the flow of three centuries. But he has pretty well demonstrated the truth of his famous saying that "one man raised by God's power to stand and live in the same spirit the prophets and apostles were in can shake the country ten miles around"—yes, for ten thousand miles, and for three centuries. He has made it easier for us to believe in the triumph of ideals, and he has verified the fact that the way of faith and love is a real way to the achievement of good ends; and it may even turn

[1] *Ibid.*, i, p. 68.

out to be the only way. His impact on the world has been, what he would have wished it to be, slow and gradual, the gentle influence of spiritual forces. He was, as William Penn said, "a heavenly minded man"; and after his long, hard, honest fight for truth and goodness, he had some right to speak those last dying words of his, "I am clear, I am fully clear."

George Fox's world was a very different one from our world today. His ideas and his hopes have such a different setting and such a peculiar fringe and background that it is not easy to dissociate them from their climate and to envisage them in the transformed light and atmosphere of this new age. Even when a man is "ahead of his time" his thoughts and projects are all valued in terms of its strivings and conflicts, not in the perspective of later centuries. The struggles, the changes, the spiritual achievements of these three centuries since George Fox learned to say "thou," have no parallel in any other three-century span of history and we must calmly recognise the fact that he belongs in the seventeenth century, not in the twentieth. He would feel far from home if he were suddenly "dropped down" into the labyrinth of our complicated life and if he found himself confronted with the maze of our "modern" questions and problems. And yet he has made a real contribution to the world of today; he has a vital message for it; his spirit and his religious insight speak in no uncertain way to our present condition, and we are at many points immense debtors to him. Not the least among his contributions to us are his personality and his own experience. George Eliot finely said:

> The greatest legacy a hero leaves his race
> Is—to have been a hero.

George Fox's overcoming life, his conquering faith, the depth and conviction of his own experience, outweigh any words he spoke. He reveals the freshness, the vitality, the staying quality of a real man. His human qualities and his odd humour are precious traits. His tempered optimism is a splendid tonic, and his inward sense that "the seed of God reigns and is over all" [1] stirs us with thanksgiving even yet.

[1] *Journal*, ii, p. 506.

CHAPTER XIII

The Character of Fox

IT WILL be fitting to say a few words to gather up the character of the man himself. George Fox was by no means free of faults and defects. He was not always inspired; he was often dull and tedious. Though usually very humble and tender, he yet sometimes was overconscious of his importance and he occasionally shared the tendency of his age to speak with an air of infallibility and finality. He felt undue satisfaction in the calamities which overtook his persecutors, though we should all admit that it is a very human trait. But when these and other necessary discounts and subtractions are made, he still stands forth a true specimen of an apostolic man and heroic reformer, absolutely sincere, honest, brave, uncompromising, and with an eye single for the light of God in his soul. Once more William Penn's pithy sentence exactly hits the truth of him: "In all things he acquitted himself like a man, yea a strong man, a new and heavenly-minded man. A divine and a naturalist, and all of God Almighty's making."

Intellectually he was not well qualified to be a reformer of Christianity. He had no clear comprehension of history. He did not understand the development of religious thought and Christian institutions, and he had slender capacity for sound interpretation of the meaning of Scripture. He knew almost nothing of the great spiritual literature of the ages. Those lacks mean, of course, a heavy handicap. He must not be judged or estimated in the class of scholarly or critical reformers. He does not belong there. He belongs in the order of the mystical, or intuitional, prophets. He is of the same general type as St. Francis of Assisi, St. Catharine of Siena, and Jacob Boehme of Silesia. The rational, reflective element was slight in the case of all these leaders. They saw the way forward without knowing dialectically the grounds or reasons for their course. They had "flashes" (that is Boehme's word) or "openings" (that is Fox's phrase). By some swift and untraceable inward leap they came to their insight and knew, as all geniuses know, that they were right.

When the "flash" was on, when the "opening" came, they were like Moses with his pillar of cloud and fire—they knew the way and they marched straight on toward their Canaan. Those who critically plot out every step and explain the grounds for every conclusion will never feel at home with this type of prophet, and they will never be satisfied with the prophet's contribution. They will list it in the class with superstition or fanaticism. It is one of those matters about which it is useless to argue. The prophet is not to be "explained"; he is to be accepted as a genius, or peradventure be passed by as unimportant and negligible. Here in this type at any rate Fox belongs. He lacked some traits which St. Francis and St. Catherine had, but he was like them in type, though he was still more closely allied to Boehme.

Fox had, as St. Francis also had, a large gift of humour. It was not a designed and conscious humour. It was a fundamental, native trait of personality as it was to such a marked degree in that old Greek prophet, Socrates. Fox always felt the humorous aspect of situations in which he found himself. Take as a specimen his account of sitting for hours in silence on a haystack with a great throng of "professors"—*i. e.*, nominal Christians—waiting for him to speak. "I sat on a haystack and spoke nothing for some hours; *for I was to famish them from words.* The 'professors' would ever and anon be speaking to the old priest, asking him when I would begin and when I would speak." [1] Here is another good passage: "One whose name was Cock met me in the street and would give me a roll of tobacco, for people were then much given to smoking. I accepted his love but did not receive his tobacco." [2] On another occasion he accepted a Ranter's offer of tobacco, as he says, "to show him that I was in unity with the creation!" [3] When he was in Derby jail a conjurer in the jail threatened "to raise the Devil and break down the house," so that the jailer was afraid. Fox says: "I was moved of the Lord to go in His power and rebuke him, and to say to him: 'Come, let us see what thou canst do; do thy worst.' I told him the Devil was raised high enough in him already; but the power of God chained him down, so he slunk away from me." [4] At another time an opponent of his doc-

[1] *Journal*, i, p. 94. [2] *Ibid.*, i, p. 116.
[3] *Ibid*. (Cambridge Edition), i, p. 44.
[4] *Ibid.*, i, p. 72.

trine cried out: "What must be damned?" And Fox says, "I was moved immediately to tell him that that which spoke in him was to be damned!" He turned the tables on Judge Glynn, the Chief Justice, who was bullying him over wearing his hat and who said, "Come, tell me where any in the Bible kept on their hats from Moses to Daniel?" by replying without a moment's hesitation, "Thou mayest read in the third of Daniel that the three children were cast into the fiery furnace by Nebuchadnezzar's command with their coats, their hose, and their hats on!" [1]

The outstanding impression which the *Journal* gives is the uncompromising bravery of the man. He could not be frightened or thrown into a panic. In this trait he is like Luther, who was determined to go to Leipzig, "even if it rained Duke Georges nine days running!" Fox was sixty times brought before the courts and eight times imprisoned, as we have seen, in jails, prisons, or castle dungeons. He was the victim of many mobs and frequently endured brutal treatment at the hands of cruel gangs of persecutors. In no instance did he show any fear nor

[1] *Journal*, i, p. 273.

did any threat ever induce him to change his line of procedure when he was obeying what he believed to be a call of duty. On one occasion a man rushed at him with a naked rapier. Fox looked steadfastly at him and said, calmly: "Alack for thee, poor creature! What will thou do with thy carnal weapon? It is no more to me than a straw." [1] After Fox had received a most terrific handling by the mob at Ulverston, a soldier, with his sword by his side, came up and said to him, "Sir, I see you are a man!" [2] The more he was threatened and challenged in any town or region the more he felt moved to go there and deliver his message. "There were," the *Journal* reports, "great threatenings given forth in Cumberland that if I ever came there they would take away my life. When I heard it I was drawn to go into Cumberland." [3] In Beaumaris, for example, people told him that if he went into the street again the magistrates and governor would imprison him and they urged him to stay quietly in his inn. "Upon this," he says, "I was moved to go and walk up and down in the streets!" [4] The officers and

[1] *Journal,* i, p. 49.
[2] *Ibid.,* i, p. 133.
[3] *Ibid.,* i, p. 159.
[4] *Ibid.,* i, p. 379.

soldiers in Scarborough Castle said of him, "He is as stiff as a tree and as pure as a bell." [1]

Fox felt himself to be sent forth on an apostolic mission and he firmly believed that on occasions he was granted miraculous power. He frequently refers to the "wonderful power" which attended his labours or which "broke forth" when he was speaking. On one occasion he says, "The power of God thundered among them"; and again, "There was a mighty dread amongst the people." In a famous passage he declared, "The Lord said unto me that if but one man or woman were raised by His Power to stand and live in the same spirit that the prophets and apostles were in who gave forth the Scriptures, that man or woman should shake the country for ten miles round," [2] and there can, I think, be no doubt that he believed himself to be a man of that type. He told the priests at Swarthmore very emphatically that he had received a message and word from the Lord as the prophets and apostles of old had done, and then he asks, "Can any of you say you have ever had a command or word from the Lord immediately at any time"? [3] In connection with

[1] *Journal*, ii, p. 70.
[2] *Journal*, i, p. 109.
[3] *Ibid.*, i, p. 127.

[211]

an early visit to Mansfield-Woodhouse he declared: "Many great and wonderful things were wrought by the heavenly power in those days; for the Lord made bare His omnipotent arm, and manifested His power, to the astonishment of many, by the healing virtue whereby many have been delivered from great infirmities." [1]

There is plain evidence in the *Journal* that Fox had a certain majesty of personality that made itself felt upon both friends and enemies as he moved about among men. He quickly became a moving and silently dominating power in any group where he was present, though there is very little indication that he strained after leadership or control. The power of his eyes was often noted and it must have been a striking feature of him, especially when he was in an exalted state under inspiration. At least four times in the *Journal* there is expressed a strong testimony to this trait of personality. The first instance reported is a fairly simple one. It occurred at Sedbergh among "the people in white raiment." "I came into a house," Fox says, "and there came in one Capt. Warde and hee saide my very eyes peirced through him and hee was convinced of God's everlasting

[1] *Ibid.*, i, p. 45.

[212]

truth." [1] The second instance comes out of his experiences in Carlisle in 1653. A Baptist deacon who was contending with Fox was moved by the Lord's power and Fox says, "I sett my eyes upon him and spake sharply to him in ye power of ye Lorde, and hee cried dont peirce me soe with thy eyes keepe thy eyes off mee." [2]

A no less impressive instance occurred on the second visit to Holland in 1684 when Fox was sixty. IIe was having a debate with Galenus Abrahams, a noted Mennonite, when the Mennonite suddenly said: "Keep your eyes off me, for they pierce me." [3]

The most memorable testimony to the striking face and personality of Fox is that given by the students at Cambridge when they were trying to pull him off his horse in rough play: "I kept on my horse's backe and ridd through them in ye Lords power: Oh saide they hee shines hee glisters." [4]

One of the most touching of all his accounts of the display of power is the one which tells how a mason who was a "professor" struck his hand with a rule-staff such a blow that the hand

[1] *Cambridge Journal*, i, p. 42.
[2] *Ibid.*, p. 115.   [3] *Journal*, ii, p. 401.
[4] *Cambridge Journal*, i, p. 190.

seemed ruined and incapable of any further use.
"But," he says, "I looked at it in the love of
God (for I was in the love of God to all that
persecuted me) and after a while the Lord's
power sprang through me again, and through
my hand and arm, so that in a moment I recovered strength in my hand and arm in the
sight of them all." [1]

The thing that saved Fox from over-exalta-
tion and from exaggerated claims was this genuine spirit of love which abounded in his soul
and a deep-seated common sense with which he
was endowed. He sometimes ran close up to the
border line of danger, and some of his followers
crossed the line, but he himself weathered the
storms and testings which beset his life and his
mission. He preserved his balance and sanity,
and for the most part he was not only valiant
and daring, but serene and wisely tempered.

I have purposely omitted the details of his
movements and labours during the years after
his return from America, except in so far as they
have come in incidentally in the Chapters on
Organisation and on Imprisonments. These last
years were burdened with heavy responsibilities,
with suffering over persecution, and with the

[1] *Journal*, i, p. 133.

sadness incident to misunderstanding and opposition within the fold. He bore all these things nobly and moved straight forward toward the completion of his work and mission with a manly heart. He met death as he had always met the sterner facts of life, with undisturbed faith and heroic spirit. A little before the end he said, "All is well; the Seed of God reigns over all, and over death itself." A short time earlier he had said, as he "felt the cold strike to his heart," "Now I am clear, I am fully clear." It is a good dying testimony and few men have had more right to say it at the close of life. His death occurred in London, January 11, 1691.

THE END

Index

[218]

Holland, 151, 213
"Holy Experiment, the," 163
Hooton, Elizabeth, 162, 167 f.
Hotham, Justice Durant, 52
Howgill, Francis, 57 ff., 87 ff., 196
Hubberthorne, Richard (of Yealand), 59
Hull, John, 162
Human Nature, Calvinistic conception of, 14
"Humanist," 30
Humanistic-mystical movement, 156
"Humiliation, day of," 81
Hyde Park, 120 f.

Imprisonment of Fox, at Derby, 49 ff., 96, 208
  at Lancaster and Scarborough, 104 ff., 133, 139, 211
  at Leicester, 104
  at London and Worcester, 108 ff., 151
  at Nottingham, 47 ff.
  in Carlisle, 96 f.
  in Lancaster Castle, 103
  in Launceston Castle, 98 ff.
Independents, 5
Indians, North American, 199
Industry, the, 162
Inner Light, Quaker doctrine of, 115, 122
Insight, "Flashes" of, 36, 206 f.

"Introverts," 23
"Inward-building," 37
Inward Light, proclamation of, 62 ff.
Irish visit, 149
Ives, St., 99

Jaffray, Alexander, 154
James I, reign of, 8
James, William, 1, 14
Jay, John, 183
Jeremiah, 76
Jesus Christ, 21
Joan of Arc, 35, 36
Journal (Fox's), 7, 9 n., 13, 14 n., 15 n., 19, 21 n., 24, 27 n., 28 n., 30 n., 33 n., 34 n., 35 n., 38, 39 n., 41, 44 n., 45, 47, 48 n., 51 n., 53 n., 56, 58, 68, 78 n., 79, 81 n., 82 n., 83 n., 85 n., 93 n., 95 n., 97 n., 98 n., 102, 104 n., 107 n., 111 f., 117, 118 n., 119 n., 121 n., 122 n., 126 n., 127, 131 n., 132 n., 136, 154, 198 n., 199 n., 201 n., 202 n., 204 n., 208 n., 209 f., 210 n., 211 n., 212, 212 n., 213 n., 214 n.

Keith, George, 41, 154
Kendal, 57
Killam Thomas, 52
Kingdom of God, 76

[220]